Weekly FAMILY Devotions

by Jason & Brenda Carr

Insignia
PUBLICATIONS

Sacramento, CA

Weekly Family Devotions
by Jason & Brenda Carr

©2013 Jason & Brenda Carr

First Printing
ISBN: 978-0-9823912-6-6
Library of Congress Control Number: 2012955523

Printed in the United States of America
All scripture quotations are taken from the Holy Bible in the following versions:
KJV (*King James Version*, Public Domain)
NASB (*New American Standard Bible*, Published by Zondervan)
NIV (*New International Version,* published by Zondervan)
NKJV (*New King James Version*, published by Thomas Nelson, Inc.)
NLT (*New Living Translation*, published by Tyndale House Publishers, Inc.)

Editing by Cynthia Carr

Published by Insignia Publications
Sacramento, California
www.InsigniaBooks.com
(916) 669-1100

For additional copies please contact Turnpoint Counseling at:
www.TurnpointCounseling.com
jcarr@turnpointcounseling.com

Dedication

This book is dedicated to our children Brooklyn and Boston Carr:

Brooklyn:

We are so thankful for the godly young lady you have become. It gives us great joy to see you at 13 years of age very involved in ministry, giving of your time and talents to the Kingdom. Your love for children's ministry and for people is amazing. You are a tremendous blessing to our ministry and to others as you minister in sign language. You are truly anointed! Thank you for your sweet spirit, we know God has great plans for your life. Let Him be the one that continually guides and orders your steps.
Always remember to keep "Jesus at the Center of it All."

Boston:

You are a joy to us! You have a love for missions, you are compassionate towards people, and sensitive to the Spirit of God. We are blessed to see you at 9 years of age be a prayer intercessor and a real giver. We have watched you during offerings give your ALL and then the next month do it all over again. You truly have a revelation of giving and we know God has blessings for you. Never lose your dreams and your tenderness to the Spirit of God. This world will have many temptations and distractions that will pull at you.
Always remember "Only Jesus Will Satisfy Your Soul."

Train up a child in the way he should go: and when he is old, he will not depart from it.   Proverbs 22:6

How To Use This Book

We are excited that you have made the choice to implement *Weekly Family Devotions* in your home! Now that you have made this decision, keep in mind that an attitude of "stick-to-it-ness" will be required. Distractions and interruptions will attempt to hinder this precious time together with your family. In our home, there have been times where it felt like we were having "Family Commotion" rather than "Family Devotion." Remember, if one week does not go as planned, don't get discouraged. Just pick up the following week where you left off. God is with you, and this time spent teaching and praying together as a family has eternal rewards!

1. According to your schedule, set aside one night each week for a time of family devotion. If possible, choose the same night each week. This will help with consistency. Plan to spend one to two hours together.

2. Spend time in prayer throughout the week for your time together.

3. Read over the devotion in advance to make sure you have all the necessary supplies for the "Family Activity."

4. Plan a family meal together to start the evening.
   - Assign responsibilities to each family member for the meal (preparation, setting the table, clean up, etc.)

5. In preparation for the devotion:
   - Have Bibles available for everyone
   - Turn off or silence all distractions (cell phone, radio, etc.)

6. Explain to the family that this time of devotion is tremendously important and that **nothing** should interfere with your time together (phone calls, text, etc.)
   Warning: Kids will not always be cooperative little angels during devotion, at times they may even be quite frustrating. **Don't give up**! There have been times, due to our children's unfavorable behavior during devotion, that they had to go to bed without dessert (or some other consequence.) This helped encourage better behavior during the next devotion.

7. Do your best to make the devotions enjoyable and fun. This will help the family look forward to the next week's "Family Devotion".

We are confidant your devotions will be time well invested and that you will never regret these special moments together as family. Our prayers are with you and your family as you embark on this journey.

Table of Contents

Table of Contents

A man ought to live so that everybody knows he is a Christian... and most of all, his family ought to know.

-D.L. Moody

Seek First His Kingdom

 ## Scripture

Take turns reading the following scriptures out loud.

Matthew 6:33; But seek first His kingdom and His righteousness, and all these things will be added to you. NASB

Proverbs 16:9; The mind of man plans his way, but the Lord directs his steps. NASB

Story: A Time for Resolutions

The New Year is an interesting time. Somehow it provides us the opportunity to forget mistakes of the past and look forward to the time that lies before us with optimism and hope. Research says that approximately 140 million people make one or more resolutions each year. That's 45% of the North American population.

Among the top New Year's resolutions are resolutions to spend more time with family, weight loss, exercise, and learning something new. Also popular are resolutions dealing with better money management or debt reduction.

The following statistics show how many resolutions are maintained as time goes on:

- Past the first week: 75%
- Past 2 weeks: 71%
- After one month: 64%
- After 6 months: 46%

While a lot of people who make New Year's resolutions do break them, research shows that making resolutions is useful. People who write down resolutions are 10 times more likely to attain their goals than people who don't write them down. 46% of individuals who wrote their resolutions down were still on track 6 months later compared to only 4% who did not write them down.

Resolutions are not something new. We can read about individuals in the Bible who made resolutions. David resolved he would not sin with his mouth by speaking wrong or damaging words. Jehoshaphat resolved to inquire of the Lord and proclaimed a fast for all of Israel. Daniel resolved not to defile himself by eating the king's food and drinking the king's wine. Paul resolved to speak only of the crucifixion of Christ Jesus and what it would mean to the Corinthians. Resolutions can be a powerful thing. When a Holy Spirit filled, child of God makes up their mind to dedicate and serve God with all their heart, soul and might there is no demon in hell that can stand in their way and stop them from achieving victory.

 **Application**

Seek First His Kingdom

1. Have a time of family prayer and devotion:
   - Praise and worship God.
   - Repentance
   - Ask for God to place a goal on your heart to complete this year.
   - Ask God to lead you in His righteousness.
   - Ask God to direct your steps.
   - Praise God for listening and answering your prayer.
2. Discuss ways each family member can improve by putting the Kingdom of God first.
   Example: A daily time of prayer and Bible reading, personal accountability partner, supporting a missionary, involvement in ministry at your local church, prayer for the lost, and a personal favorite - commitment to a weekly time of family devotion.
3. Write down two goals for each family member for the year.
4. Post the goals in a place where everyone can see.

 **Family Activity**

Hide and Seek

Pick a place in the house (chair or couch) that can be home base (the safe spot). One person counts to 25 while everyone else hides throughout the house. When the person who is "it" gets done counting they have to find everyone who is hiding. Anyone who makes it back to base without being tagged is safe. The person "it" must find everyone who is still hiding until everyone is either safe or has been tagged. The last person to be tagged is "it" for the next game.

Blessing in Serving

Scripture

Take turns reading the following scriptures out loud.

Matthew 23:11-12; [11] "But the greatest among you shall be your servant. [12] Whoever exalts himself shall be humbled; and whoever humbles himself shall be exalted. NASB

Matthew 25:34-40; [34] Then the King will say to those on his right, Come, you who are blessed by my Father, inherit the Kingdom prepared for you from the creation of the world. [35] For I was hungry, and you fed me. I was thirsty, and you gave me a drink. I was a stranger, and you invited me into your home. [36] I was naked, and you gave me clothing. I was sick, and you cared for me. I was in prison, and you visited me.

[37] Then these righteous ones will reply, Lord, when did we ever see you hungry and feed you? Or thirsty and give you something to drink? [38] Or a stranger and show you hospitality? Or naked and give you clothing? [39] When did we ever see you sick or in prison and visit you?

[40] And the King will say, I tell you the truth, when you did it to one of the least of these my brothers and sisters, you were doing it to me! NASB

Story: Keep Serving

The great violinist, Niccolo Paganini willed his marvelous violin to the city of Genoa on condition that it must never be played. The wood of such an instrument, while used and handled, wears only slightly, but set aside, it begins to decay. Paganini's lovely violin has today become worm-eaten and useless except as a relic.

Have you ever been to a restaurant where the server does not bring what you want? Instead, they serve you what they want to bring. A good server is someone who brings you what you ask for and is attentive to anything you might need throughout the meal. Being a good servant requires us to put our wants and needs aside and focus on the needs of those we are serving. Our spirit, just like Paganini's precious violin, will become rotten and useless unless we allow the hands of the Lord to use it and direct as He desires.

A Spanish philosopher tells about the Roman aqueduct at Segovia, Spain. It was built in 109 A.D. For eighteen hundred years, it carried cool water from the mountains to the hot and thirsty city. Nearly sixty generations of men drank from its flow. Then came another generation, who said, "This aqueduct is so great a marvel that it ought to be preserved for our children, as a museum piece. We shall relieve it of its centuries-long labor."

So they did; the workers laid modern iron pipes. They gave the ancient bricks and mortar a reverent rest. And the aqueduct began to fall apart. The sun beating on the dry mortar caused it to crumble. The bricks and stone sagged and threatened to fall. What ages of service could not destroy, idleness disintegrated. Like Paganini's violin and the Roman aqueduct, a Christian's willingness to serve and be used by God will be the thing that preserves us in our Christian walk.

Ref.: J.K. Laney, *Marching Orders*, p. 34.
Resource, Sept./ Oct., 1992, p. 4.

 **Application**

Blessing in Serving

1. Have a time of family prayer and devotion:
   - Thank and praise God for His goodness.
   - Repentance
2. Pray for each family member one at a time.
   - Have them name one prayer request for themselves and one for someone else.
   - Lay hands on them while you pray for their requests.
3. Ask God to direct your family to serve someone else within the community or the church this week. (Be still and listen for a couple of minutes then discuss who God put on your mind).
4. Praise God for listening and answering your prayer.

 Family Activity

Plan to Serve

People are happier when they serve others.
Choose an individual or family you can serve this coming week.
   - Make a plan to follow through with serving (who, what, when, and how).
   - Discuss ways each family member can be involved in this ministry opportunity.
   - Ideas: Take someone to lunch, prepare a meal or dessert and invite them to your home for fellowship, help work in their yard, or help with repairs to their home, etc..

Faithful Servant

 Scripture
Take turns reading the following scriptures out loud.

Matthew 25:23; His lord said to him, 'Well done, good and faithful servant; you have been faithful over a few things, I will make you ruler over many things. Enter into the joy of your lord.' NKJV

Proverbs 21:5; Good planning and hard work lead to prosperity, but hasty shortcuts lead to poverty. NIV

Story: A Call to Be Faithful

A famous American Senator tells of touring Calcutta with Mother Teresa and visiting the so-called "House of Dying", where sick children are cared for in their last days, and the dispensary, where the poor line up by the hundreds to receive medical attention. Watching Mother Teresa minister to these people, feeding and nursing those left by others to die, the Senator was overwhelmed by the sheer magnitude of the suffering Mother Teresa and her co-workers faced daily. "How can you bear the load without being crushed by it?" the Senator asked. Mother Teresa replied, "My dear Senator, I am not called to be successful, I am called to be faithful."

The responsibility we have to be faithful is the foundation for every area of our life. The example Jesus gave to use was an example of faithfulness, not success. Success came as a result of His faithfulness, and so will it be for you. God wants you to be faithful with the most valuable things he has placed in your life: relationships. People are more important that possessions. We may be able to replace lost or broken possessions, but never lost or broken relationships.

According to a study of more than 500 family counselors, the following are the top traits of successful families:

- Communicating and listening
- Affirming and supporting family members
- Respecting one another
- Developing a sense of trust
- Sharing time and responsibility
- Knowing right from wrong
- Having rituals and traditions
- Sharing a religious core
- Respecting privacy

God desires you to have success in your life and in your relationships. Being faithful means I go beyond just talking about what needs to change and actually plan and implement the change that is necessary. Faithfulness is the first step towards tomorrow's success.

Ref.: *Focus on the Family Bulletin*, December, 1988

 **Application**

Faithful Servant

1. Have a time of family prayer and devotion:
   - Praise and worship God.
   - Repentance
   - Ask God to show you areas from the story that your family needs to improve in.
   - Ask God for His wisdom and direction to improve your faithfulness.
   - Praise God for listening and answering your prayer.
2. Open up to one another regarding areas you have slipped in your faithfulness towards each other.
3. Discuss ways each family member can improve in being faithful towards each other.

 **Family Activity**

Puzzle Time

Work on a puzzle as a family.

Choose a puzzle that will take approximately 20 to 30 minutes to piece together (younger kids will lose interest if it takes too long).

Divide up the pieces of the puzzle evenly to each family member regardless of age.

Each person must be responsible for connecting their piece to the puzzle. Younger children may need assistance in finding the proper location, but make sure they are the one to connect the pieces from their pile.

Activity Discussion:

Just as each family member had the responsibility of working on the puzzle to complete it, each person has a responsibility to the family as a unit.

Each person had different pieces of the puzzle and had to use their pieces to complete the puzzle. Each family member has different talents and abilities they contribute to the family to make it complete.

Faithfulness requires effort, commitment, and persistence. A successful family requires each member to have the same characteristics.

Love of God

Scripture

Take turns reading the following scriptures out loud.

Deuteronomy 7:9; Understand, therefore, that the Lord your God is indeed God. He is the faithful God who keeps his covenant for a thousand generations and lavishes his unfailing love on those who love him and obey his commands. NLT

Psalm 51:1; Have mercy on me, O God, according to your unfailing love; according to your great compassion blot out my transgressions. NIV

John 3:16; For God so loved the world, that he gave his only begotten Son, that whosoever believeth in him should not perish, but have everlasting life. KJV

Story: Unconditional Love

In order for parents to love their children effectively they must remember that (1) They are children. (2) They tend to act like children. (3) Much of childish behavior is unpleasant. (4) If you do your part as a parent and love them despite their childish behavior, they will be able to mature and give up childish ways. (5) If you only love them when they please you (conditional love), and convey your love to them only during these times, they will not feel genuinely loved. This in turn will make them insecure, damage their self-image, and actually prevent them from moving on to better self-control and more mature behavior. Therefore, their behavior is your responsibility as much as theirs. (6) If you love them unconditionally, they will feel good about themselves and be comfortable with themselves. This will help them be able to control their anxiety and behavior, as they grow into adulthood.

All of us, regardless of age, are God's children. He knows who we are. He knows our strengths and weaknesses. He knows everything about us and He loves us unconditionally. His love for us is greater than we could ever imagine. Jesus stated in Matthew 7:9; "Which of you, if his son ask for bread, will give him a stone? Or if he asks for a fish, will give him a snake? If you, then, though you are evil, know how to give good gifts to your children, how much more will your Father in heaven give good gifts to those who ask Him!" Only when we pass between the pearly gates, walk upon streets of pure gold, and bow down before His throne in honor and reverence will we even begin to understand the depths of His love.

God left the splendor and majesty of heaven and became human so He might pave the way for you and I to know what true love is. There is nothing you can do to make God love you more! There is nothing you can do to make God love you less! His love is Unconditional, Impartial, Everlasting, Infinite, and Perfect!

Ref.: Dr. Ross Campbell, *How to Really Love Your Child.*

 <u>**Application**</u>

Love of God

1. Have a time of family prayer and devotion:
   - Praise and worship God.
   - Repentance
   - Ask God to show you things that might be cluttering your heart and making it difficult for Him to live there.
   - Ask God to remove the clutter from your heart and life.
   - Pray for each family member one at a time.
   - Have them name one prayer request for themselves and one for a new Christian.
   - Lay hands on them while you pray for their requests.
2. Ask God to reveal the depth of His love in your life this week.
3. Ask God to help you love those in your family unconditionally.
4. Discuss actions you can perform to show your family members unconditional love.

 <u>**Family Activity**</u>

What's in the Heart

You will need the following items:
   - Blank paper
   - Crayons / markers
   - Old magazines

Draw a large heart on your blank piece of paper.
   - Cut out pictures from the magazine that depict what is valuable or fun to them (actions, possessions, words, etc.)
   - Have each family member explain what their picture means and why they placed the items in their heart.
   - Paul gives instruction in 1 Timothy 1:5; The purpose of my instruction is that all believers would be filled with love that comes from a pure heart, a clear conscience, and genuine faith.
   - Discuss how things of this world can clutter our hearts. Most of the items may not represent something wrong, but we need to ensure there is plenty of room for God to live and dwell within us.
   - God desires to live within a heart that is not cluttered with things of this world. God will not live in a heart full of sin.
   - Is there anything in your heart that must be cleaned out or repented of so God can make your heart His home?

Love Thy Enemy

 Scripture

Take turns reading the following scriptures out loud.

Leviticus 19: 16-18; [16]Do not spread slanderous gossip among your people. Do not stand idly by when your neighbor's life is threatened. I am the Lord. [17]Do not nurse hatred in your heart for any of your relatives. Confront people directly so you will not be held guilty for their sin. [18]Do not seek revenge or bear a grudge against a fellow Israelite, but love your neighbor as yourself. I am the Lord. NLT

Matthew 5:43-48; [43]You have heard that it was said, You shall love your neighbor and hate your enemy. [44]But I say to you, love your enemies and pray for those who persecute you, [45] so that you may be sons of your Father who is in heaven; for He causes His sun to rise on the evil and the good, and sends rain on the righteous and the unrighteous. [46]For if you love those who love you, what reward do you have? Do not even the tax collectors do the same? [47]If you greet only your brothers, what more are you doing than others? Do not even the Gentiles do the same? [48]Therefore you are to be perfect, as your heavenly Father is perfect. NLT

Story: You Want Me to Love Who?

A reporter was interviewing an elderly man on his 100th birthday. "What are you most proud of?" he asked. "Well," said the man, "I don't have an enemy in the world." "What a beautiful thought! How inspirational!" said the reporter. "Yep," added the elderly man, "I outlived every last one of them."

Peter Miller, who was a Baptist pastor during the American Revolution, lived in Ephrata, Pennsylvania, and enjoyed the friendship of George Washington. In Ephrata also lived Michael Wittman, an evil-minded individual who did all he could to oppose and humiliate the pastor. One day Michael Wittman was arrested for treason and sentenced to die. Pastor Peter Miller traveled seventy miles on foot to Philadelphia to plead for the life of the traitor. "No, Peter," General Washington said. "I cannot grant you the life of your friend." "My friend!" exclaimed the old preacher. "He's the bitterest enemy I have." "What?" cried Washington.

"You've walked seventy miles to save the life of an enemy? That puts the matter in different light. I'll grant your pardon." And he did. Pastor Peter Miller took Michael Wittman back home to Ephrata - no longer an enemy but a friend.

"It is easy enough to be friendly to one's friends. But to befriend the one who regards himself as your enemy is the essence of true religion. The other is mere business." – Gandhi

Reasons why you should love your enemies:
- You'll be happier.
- You could change that person's life.
- You could make a friend.
- You set a better example for others.
- It's better for society.
- It's a test for you as a person.

"Love is the only force capable of transforming an enemy into friend." - Martin Luther King Jr.

 <u>**Application**</u>

Love Thy Enemy

Have a time of family prayer and devotion.

1. Discuss the following scripture in light of the story and Matthew 6:14-15; [14]"If you forgive those who sin against you, your heavenly Father will forgive you. [15]But if you refuse to forgive others, your Father will not forgive your sins".

2. Discuss openly about those who have offended or hurt you.
   - If necessary write down the names of those you need to forgive.
   - Pray for them one at a time and ask God to help you forgive them for what they have done.
   - Once you have forgiven others, ask God to forgive you of any sins and wrongs you have done to other people.
   - Ask God to bless the people in your life that you find difficult to love.

Ten Tips For Loving Your Enemy:
1. Stop, breathe, and detach yourself

2. Put yourself in their shoes

3. Seek to understand

4. Seek to accept

5. Forgive, and let the past go

6. Find something to love

7. See them as yourself, or a loved one

8. Find common ground

9. Open your heart

10. Reach out to them

 <u>**Family Activity**</u>

Ice Cream Night

Either go out and get individual scoops at the local ice cream shop or grab a ½ gallon to bring home. Let the kids pick the flavor.
Spend time sitting around talking as you indulge in the tasty treat.

To Love Is to Serve

Scripture

Take turns reading the following scriptures out loud.

Deuteronomy 10:12; Now, Israel, what does the Lord your God require from you, but to fear the Lord your God, to walk in all His ways and love Him, and to serve the Lord your God with all your heart and with all your soul. NASB

Matthew 6:24; No one can serve two masters; for either he will hate the one and love the other, or he will be devoted to one and despise the other. You cannot serve God and wealth. NASB

Story: Reach Out and Touch Someone

"Whoever loves much, does much. It is natural to love them that love us, but it is supernatural to love them that hate us." (Source unknown)

The absence of parental affection is tremendously detrimental to children. Just how damaging it can be is revealed in a study done in a South American orphanage. Researchers observed and recorded what happened to 97 children who were deprived of emotional and physical contact with others. Because of a lack of funds, there was not enough staff to adequately care for these children, ages 3 months to 3 years old. Nurses changed diapers and fed and bathed the children, but there was little time to hold, cuddle, or talk to them as a mother would. After three months, many of them showed signs of abnormality. Besides a loss of appetite and being unable to sleep well, many of the children lay with a vacant expression in their eyes. After five months, serious deterioration set in.

They lay whimpering, with troubled and twisted faces. Often, when a doctor or nurse would pick up an infant, it would scream in terror. Twenty seven, almost one third, of the children died the first year, but not from lack of food or health care. They died from a lack of touch and emotional nurture. Because of this, several more died the second year. Only twenty-one of the 97 survived most suffering serious psychological damage.

Both the Apostle Peter and the Apostle Paul make reference to new Christians as babes in Christ. New Christians need to be nurtured and cared for so they may grow in spiritual and relational stature with God. Do you ever wonder why new Christians stop coming to church? I think the deeper question is, "Have you reached out and nurtured them, touched them, taken the time to talk to them, and shown them the affection of God?" Our love for God drives us to serve Him. Our love for Him drives us to serve His people. We should display our love by taking personal responsibility to reach and touch these babes in Christ so they will not only survive but thrive within the body of Christ.

> He prays best who loves best
> All things both great and small;
> For the dear God who loves us,
> He made and loves us all.
> –Samuel T. Coleridge.

Ref.: Charles Sell, *Unfinished Business*, Multnomah, 1989, p. 39.

Application

To Love Is to Serve

1. Have a time of family prayer and devotion:
   - Praise and worship God.
   - Repentance
2. Pray for each family member one at a time.
3. Have them name one prayer request for themselves and one for a new Christian.
4. Lay hands on them while you pray for their requests.
5. Ask God to direct your family to reach out to a new person in the church, to be God's voice, hands, and heart in caring for this new babe in Christ.
6. Praise God for listening and answering your prayer.

Family Activity

Pick a Person

Discuss ways you can encourage, nurture, talk to, and care for the individual you prayed for earlier. Each family member should have a different person.

Focus on getting outside of your world and into theirs:
- Send them a note, card, text, e-mail, or letter.
- Call them when they miss a service and let them know you missed them.
- Schedule a time to get together and have fun.
- Invite them to small groups that operate within the church and help them meet others.

Attitude of Holiness

Scripture

Take turns reading the following scriptures out loud.

1 Samuel 16:7; But the Lord said to Samuel, "Don't judge by his appearance or height, for I have rejected him. The Lord doesn't see things the way you see them. People judge by outward appearance, but the Lord looks at the heart." NLT

Ephesians 1:18; pray that your hearts will be flooded with light so that you can understand the confident hope he has given to those he called—his holy people who are his rich and glorious inheritance. NLT

1 Thessalonians 3:12-13; [12]And may the Lord make your love for one another and for all people grow and overflow, just as our love for you overflows. [13]May he, as a result, make your hearts strong, blameless, and holy as you stand before God our Father when our Lord Jesus comes again with all his holy people. Amen. NLT

Story: Attitude = Altitude

A truly humble man is hard to find, yet God delights to honor such selfless people. Booker T. Washington, the renowned black educator, was an outstanding example of this truth. Shortly after he took over the presidency of Tuskegee Institute in Alabama, he was walking in an exclusive section of town when he was stopped by a wealthy white woman. Not knowing the famous Mr. Washington by sight, she asked if he would like to earn a few dollars by chopping wood for her. Because he had no pressing business at the moment, Professor Washington smiled, rolled up his sleeves, and proceeded to do the humble chore she had requested. When he was finished, he carried the logs into the house and stacked them by the fireplace. A little girl recognized him and later revealed his identity to the lady.

The next morning the embarrassed woman went to see Mr. Washington in his office at the Institute and apologized profusely. "It's perfectly all right, Madam," he replied. "Occasionally I enjoy a little manual labor. Besides, it's always a delight to do something for a friend." She shook his hand warmly and assured him his meek and gracious attitude had endeared him and his work to her heart. Not long afterward she showed her admiration by persuading some wealthy acquaintances to join her in donating thousands of dollars to the Tuskegee Institute.

Holiness is not just looking the part, but living the part. Living a holy life is every bit a proper attitude towards others as it is having a holy and modest appearance. Have you ever seen a piece of fruit that looked so delightful and tasty that you just had to take a bite? Only to be highly disappointed and somewhat embarrassed, when you picked it up to take a bite, because it was made out of plastic. That is exactly what people who dress holy and modest are like to this world when their attitudes are rotten and ungodly. There is a proper attitude that must accompany holiness. Paul prayed for the Church in Thessalonica "may the Lord make your love for one another and for all people grow and overflow…13 May he, as a result, make your hearts strong, blameless, and holy." Holiness requires us to maintain both the right attitude and the right appearance. We represent Him! We need to stop and ask ourselves regularly "Is my attitude a good reflection of God's love and kindness? Or am I just like a fake piece of fruit, plastic and good only to look at from a distance." Mr. Washington was able to win a friend and ultimately a new disciple to his cause by letting his heart set the example of kindness and humility. Live holy, inside and out!

 **Application**

Attitude of Holiness

1. Have a time of family prayer and devotion.
2. Why is it necessary to have the right attitude?
3. What does the statement "Attitude determines altitude mean?"
4. Is the following statement true? "Everything can be taken from a man but one thing: To choose one's attitude in any given set of circumstances, to choose one's way." -Viktor Frankl
5. During your prayer time ask God to help you with your attitude especially around other family members.
6. Use Paul's prayer as a guide: 1 Thessalonians 3:12-13; [12]And may the Lord make your love for one another and for all people grow and overflow… [13]May he, as a result, make your hearts strong, blameless, and holy as you stand before God our Father when our Lord Jesus comes again with all his holy people. Amen

 **Family Activity**

Charades

Act out different attitudes that a person can have. The first one to guess correctly gets to go next.

This next activity may be difficult for younger children:
- Verbalize one emotion or attitude while acting out the opposite.
  (Example: verbally sound concerned that someone might be hurt or sick while grabbing them and pushing them around in a rough manner.)
- Yell in a harsh manner the words "I love you!" while smiling and acting kind.

Discuss how odd it is to say one thing while acting out another. Compare this to looking holy on the outside but having an unholy attitude.

Love

Scripture

Take turns reading the following scriptures out loud.

Matthew 22:37-40; [37]And He said to him, You shall love the Lord your God with all your heart, and with all your soul, and with all your mind. [38]This is the great and foremost commandment. [39]The second is like it, You shall love your neighbor as yourself. [40]On these two commandments depend the whole Law and the Prophets. NASB

John 15:13; Greater love hath no man than this, that a man lay down his life for his friends. KJV

Romans 8:35; And we know that in all things God works for the good of those who love him, who have been called according to his purpose. NASB

Story: I Love You

She was lying on the ground. In her arms she held a tiny baby girl. As I put a cooked sweet potato into her outstretched hand, I wondered if she would live until morning. Her strength was almost gone, but her tired eyes acknowledged my gift. The sweet potato could help so little . . . but it was all I had.

Taking a bite she chewed it carefully. Then, placing her mouth over her baby's mouth, she forced the soft warm food into the tiny throat. Although the mother was starving, she used the entire potato to keep her baby alive. Exhausted from her effort, she dropped her head on the ground and closed her eyes. In a few minutes the baby was asleep. I later learned that during the night the mother's heart stopped, but her little girl lived.

Love is a costly thing. True love will cause a person to give all they have to supply the needs of another. God gave the greatest example for you and I when He offered His own life for generations of people not yet even born. He loved us then, and He loves us now. His love has never faded and it never will. The problem most of us have is we take God's precious love for granted. We neglect the greatest thing in our life because it didn't cost us anything. It was a gift! Like the infant in the story, we find ourselves unable to comprehend the sacrifice that God paid so we might have eternal life. Only by following His divine example of loving others more than we love ourselves can we begin to grasp the concept of true love. When true love grips our hearts, we will find ourselves willing to give anything to care and provide for those we love, even the willingness to lay down our own lives for them.

In his book Mere Christianity, C.S. Lewis wrote, "Do not waste your time bothering whether you 'love' your neighbor act as if you did. As soon as we do this, we find one of the great secrets. When you are behaving as if you loved someone, you will presently come to love them. If you injure someone you dislike, you will find yourself disliking them more. If you do them a good turn, you will find yourself disliking them less."

Application

Love

1. Have a time of family prayer and devotion:
   - Praise and worship God.
   - Repentance
2. Ask God to forgive you for taking Him and His love for granted.
3. Ask God to forgive you for taking family members and friends for granted.
4. Pray for each family member one at a time.
   - Have them name one prayer request for themselves and one for a family member or friend that they carry a burden for.
   - Lay hands on them while you pray for their requests.
5. Ask God to reveal the depth of His love in your life this week.
6. Ask God to help you love those in your family and others unconditionally.
7. Discuss actions you can take to begin showing God and others you love and appreciate them.

Family Activity

Valentine's Dinner and Treats

Valentine's Day is the perfect time to say "I Love You" especially to your kids or grandkids! One of my fondest memories of Valentine's Day was the special dinner my mom would make each year. For this meal she would fix up the table extra fancy with Valentine decorations. The dinner would be festive, including red sauce of some kind to fit the color scheme. This was always such a special time as I could see mom take time out of her very busy schedule to prepare a fabulous dinner, set a beautiful table that included cards and little gifts for everyone in the family! We could feel the love! Now, years later my kids are asking me, "Momma, Momma are we going to have our special Valentine Dinner?" Of course we are!! This is now one of their favorite meals of the year!

- Take the time to prepare a special Valentine's family meal. Each member of the family should pitch in to help as much as possible so one person doesn't carry the entire burden of the meal, preparation, and clean up. P.S. Don't forget dessert!
- Before the meal begins each family member will need to present a special token of their love and appreciation to the other family members. You can write a letter, buy or make a card, or purchase a small gift. Before the item is opened, the family member who is giving the item will tell that person what they mean to them and how much they love and appreciate that person. This is also a good opportunity for the individual to apologize if they have mistreated them or taken them for granted.

Building Fences

Scripture

Take turns reading the following scriptures out loud.

1 Peter 2:9; But you are a chosen race, a royal Priesthood, a Holy nation, a people for God's own possession, so that you may proclaim the excellencies of Him who has called you out of darkness into His marvelous light; NASB

Leviticus 19:1-2; [1]The Lord also said to Moses, [2]Give the following instructions to the entire community of Israel. You must be holy because I, the Lord your God, am holy. NLT

Deuteronomy 7:6; For you are a holy people, who belong to the Lord your God. Of all the people on earth, the Lord your God has chosen you to be his own special treasure. NLT

Story: Beware of Dangerous Cliffs

A small town situated on a mountain top was facing a very unique problem. Just outside of the west side of town was a steep cliff. The view was spectacular. There at the edge of the horizon was a spectacular city, and at sunset the colorful display of city lights drew many to the edge of the western cliff to partake of the view. The young people of the town were particularly drawn to look upon the distant lights and wonder what pleasantries that distant city might offer. After all, the town they lived in was, from their perspective, not as bright and shiny and had become quite boring and restraining. As the youth stood looking at the distant city lights, they would become entranced and lose their balance. Several had fallen off of the steep cliff edge and were either severely hurt or died before help could arrive.

The town leaders called a meeting to discuss ways to stop their youth, whom they loved dearly, from falling off of the cliff. The debate went on for hours. The only thing the leaders of the town could agree on was there was no way of stopping the youth from admiring the lights of the distant city. After all, they stood and admired the lights when they were young, but as time went on, the allure of the city became more entrancing, enticing, and dangerous. One person suggested a health clinic be built at the bottom of the cliff to provide aid to those who had fallen. That idea was shot down because it would cost too much money and some youth may die from the fall alone. Another suggested they assign adults to stand near the edge of the cliff and pass out literature discussing the dangers of falling off the cliff. Finally, one wise gentleman stood up and suggested a simple fence be built several feet from the cliffs edge to keep youth from getting dangerously close. "What if the youth simply jump the fence?" asked one of the town's folk. "Then they will still have a few feet to go before they choose to fall to their doom," said the wise old man.

Standards of holiness can be looked at as fences placed in our lives to protect us. The world has a seductive allure that can entrance us, causing us to lose our balance, and fall into sin. The reason a standard, or fence, has been put in place is because there are dangers that exist on the other side of the fence. It is wise for a fence to be built several feet from the edge of danger so those who still insist on jumping over may see the error of their judgment and return to safety. Many times young people view a holiness standard as restraining, and an attempt by leadership, parents, and others to control their youthful zest for life. What you need to realize is that holiness standards are there to protect you from being hurt. The spirits of this world desire to steal, kill, and destroy your life and personal value. Once you have fallen off the cliff, if not killed, you will be greatly damaged and hurt. The journey back from the bottom of the cliff is very difficult, can be very painful, and take a very long time. It's wiser to stand on the safe side of the fence and trust spiritual leaders who place fences in our lives.

Building Fences

1. Have a time of family prayer and devotion.

2. Discuss holiness standards that your church has placed in your life and discuss why they are there.
   - It is important to know why the fence is there or else lack of understanding leads to rebellion.

3. Find scripture to support standards of holiness if there is a lack of clarity. (If need be, ask your pastor or pastoral staff for guidance.)

4. Ask the question, "Are there areas in our life where we have climbed over the fence of protection and stand dangerously close to the edge?"
   - If so, talk about it and make a decision about what needs to change.
   - Keep in mind both scripture and church teaching when making decisions in this area.
   - Are there things you need to remove from your home? If so, do a little Spiritual Spring Cleaning!

5. Have a time of family repentance. Submit your personal opinions and will to God and the Word of God.

6. Pray for each other individually for personal strength and a right spirit to stay away from the edge of the cliff.

 **Family Activity**

Family Walk and Talk

As you walk point out fences in your neighborhood. Why are they there? Are they designed to keep things in or out? Come up with fun ideas as to what might be behind the fence that needs to be protected? Point out various things in your neighborhood that are used to prevent accidents or protect people or animals. What might happen if these protections were not in place?

Holiness on the Inside

 ## Scripture
Take turns reading the following scriptures out loud.

Matthew 23:25-28; [25]What sorrow awaits you teachers of religious law and you Pharisees. Hypocrites! For you are so careful to clean the outside of the cup and the dish, but inside you are filthy—full of greed and self-indulgence! [26]You blind Pharisee! First wash the inside of the cup and the dish, and then the outside will become clean, too. [27]What sorrow awaits you teachers of religious law and you Pharisees. Hypocrites! For you are like whitewashed tombs—beautiful on the outside but filled on the inside with dead people's bones and all sorts of impurity. [28]Outwardly you look like righteous people, but inwardly your hearts are filled with hypocrisy and lawlessness. NASB

Psalm 1:1-3; [1]How blessed is the man who does not walk in the counsel of the wicked, Nor stand in the path of sinners, Nor sit in the seat of scoffers! [2]But his delight is in the law of the Lord, And in His law he meditates day and night. [3]He will be like a tree firmly planted by streams of water, which yields its fruit in its season and its leaf does not wither; and in whatever he does, he prospers. NASB

Story: What Would Jesus Do?

Two students were walking along a street in the Whitechapel district of London, a section where old and used clothing is sold. A fairly attractive suit hung on a rack in the window of one of the stores. On it was a sign that read: "SLIGHTLY SOILED -- GREATLY REDUCED IN PRICE."

"That's it exactly," commented one of the students. "We get soiled simply by living in a world full of sin. There are vulgar pictures on freeway signs, Internet ads, television programming, almost everywhere we look. Books and magazines portray filthy and immoral life styles, and provide tasty morsels of sin for our sinful nature. By allowing ourselves a little indulgence in dishonest or lustful thoughts, we greatly reduce our value when the time comes for our character to be appraised. Our purity and our strength are gone. We become just another piece of the general, soiled attire of this world." Yes, continual slight deviations from the path of

what's right may greatly reduce our usefulness to God and our fellowman. In fact, little secret sins can weaken our character so much that when we face a moral crisis, we may not be able to pass the test placed before us. As a result, we go down in spiritual defeat because we have been careless about little sins.

We take such great care to make sure everything looks great on the outside, that everyone around us still holds us in high esteem, but Jesus knows the condition of the inside of the vessel. Jesus was talking to the religious leaders when he said, "First wash the inside of the cup and the dish, and then the outside will become clean too." It is possible to get so caught up in what others think that we lose sight of the One we are trying to please by living holy, separated lives. Holiness must begin on the inside! When we have our motives right, when we love God and desire to please Him, there are no sacrifices we will not be willing to pay for our Savior and King!

Holiness on the Inside

1. Discuss the things in your world (school, work, home) that are unclean or impure. What influences from the world do you notice as you travel around, surf the web, or listen to the radio.
2. How might these things affect you?
3. Is it possible for these worldly influences to affect you without being fully aware of their influence?
    *   Do we become desensitized to things that were once ungodly and immoral because the world calls them normal now?
    *   Do we now accept the labels of "personal choice" when years ago the same action had the label of sin?
    *   Do we justify wrong behavior, words, or actions because other people don't have a problem with them?
    *   Do we refuse to make a stand against something we know is wrong because we now do everything possible to avoid the label of being judgmental?
4. Have a time of prayer and ask God to help keep you pure and unstained from the world around us.
    *   Ask God to wash and purify you not just on the outside, but also the inside.

 Family Activity

Judge the Ads

Go through a magazine you have in your home and see how many advertisements represent something that goes against a Christian family life style.
*   Would Jesus be happy with you promoting that particular product?
*   Would Jesus be happy with you dressing that way to promote that product?
*   Let the children give their opinions first.
*   Create your own commercial/advertisement. Dress up and use props to promote a product or business that Jesus would be proud of.
*   See who can come up with the funniest, strangest and most exciting commercial.

Holiness

Scripture

Take turns reading the following scriptures out loud.

Matthew 5:13-16; [13]You are the salt of the earth; but if the salt has become tasteless, how can it be made salty again? It is no longer good for anything, except to be thrown out and trampled under-foot by men. [14]You are the light of the world. A city set on a hill cannot be hidden; [15]nor does anyone light a lamp and put it under a basket, but on the lampstand, and it gives light to all who are in the house. [16]Let your light shine before men in such a way that they may see your good works, and glorify your Father who is in heaven. NASB

1 Timothy 3:8-10; [8]Therefore I want the men in every place to pray, lifting up holy hands, without wrath and dissension. [9]Likewise, I want women to adorn themselves with proper clothing, modestly and discreetly, not with braided hair and gold or pearls or costly garments, [10]but rather by means of good works, as is proper for women making a claim to godliness. NASB

Story: Let Your Light Shine

Two battleships assigned to the training squadron had been at sea on maneuvers in heavy weather for several days. The visibility was poor with patchy fog, so the captain remained on the bridge keeping an eye on all activities.

Shortly after dark, the lookout on the wing reported, "Light, bearing on the starboard bow."

"Is it steady or moving astern?", the captain called out.

The lookout replied, "Steady, Captain," which meant we were on a dangerous collision course with that ship.

The captain then called to the signalman, "Signal that ship: We are on a collision course, advise you change course twenty degrees."

Back came the signal, "Advisable for you to change course twenty degrees."

The captain said, "Send: I'm a captain, change course twenty degrees."

"I'm a seaman second-class," came the reply. "You had better change course twenty degrees."

By that time the captain was furious. He spat out, "Send: I'm a battleship. Change course twenty degrees, or you will be blown out of the water!"

Back came the flashing light, "I'm a lighthouse, your move."

The battleship changed course.

D.L. Moody once said, "A holy life will make the deepest impression. Lighthouses blow no horns, they just shine." Jesus told his followers that they were the light of the world. Two thousand years later we are still the light of the world. God does not want us to hide or be ashamed of our holiness and dedication unto him. He wants the entire world to see us! We are His chosen people. Like the battleship, the world tries to tell us to change our course, to be like them, dress, talk, and act like them. Like the lighthouse, we stand firm on the foundation that God created for us and cry out, "We are the light of the world! There is no moving an unmovable truth!" We dress, act, and talk the way we do to please the Lord. If we were looking for worldly approval we would be like the world, but the applause we desire to hear is the applause of nail scarred hands. Let your light shine for all the world to see, and continue to direct the lost toward the Savior.

I would not give much for your religion unless it can be seen. Lamps do not talk, but they do shine.

 **Application**

Holiness

1. Have a time of family prayer and devotion.

2. Ask God to forgive you if you have been judgmental of others according to their outward appearance.

3. Ask God to help you be a living example of His holiness before others.
   - Ask God to help you be more concerned about what He thinks than what this world thinks.

4. Have a family discussion regarding holiness and what can be done to ensure that this world can see the light of Jesus in you.

5. Is there anything in your life that you feel needs to change so that you can be a better witness for the Lord?
   - If so talk about it and make a decision about what needs to be done.
   - Keep in mind both scripture and church teaching when making decisions in this area.

 **Family Activity**

Flashlight Tag

- Turn most of the lights off in the house.
- One person gets a flashlight while the rest of the family runs.
- When the light hits someone they are it.

Notice how difficult it is to get around safely without the light, while the one with the flashlight has no problems at all finding their way around safely.

Compare this to walking in this world without the light of Jesus shining through us. It's His light that will help lead us through difficult and dangerous times.

End Times

 ## Scripture

Take turns reading the following scriptures out loud.

Matthew 24:1-8; [1]As Jesus was leaving the Temple grounds, his disciples pointed out to him the various Temple buildings. [2]But he responded, "Do you see all these buildings? I tell you the truth, they will be completely demolished. Not one stone will be left on top of another!"

[3]Later, Jesus sat on the Mount of Olives. His disciples came to him privately and said, "Tell us, when will all this happen? What sign will signal your return and the end of the world?"

[4]Jesus told them, "Don't let anyone mislead you, [5]for many will come in my name, claiming, 'I am the Messiah.' They will deceive many. [6]And you will hear of wars and threats of wars, but don't panic. Yes, these things must take place, but the end won't follow immediately. [7]Nation will go to war against nation, and kingdom against kingdom. There will be famines and earthquakes in many parts of the world. [8]But all this is only the first of the birth pains, with more to come. NLT

Story: Are You Ready?

As the lights dimmed there was an eerie silence that fell over the entire congregation. Suddenly a tremendous roar shook the entire building. I could feel sound waves reverberating through my chest as I sat in total darkness. My heart leapt with fear realizing this was what the end would sound like for me if I missed the rapture, the second coming of the Lord Jesus Christ! I was attending an End Time Prophecy crusade held by a prominent minister who specialized in end time teaching and preaching. During his presentation he showed numerous slides to aid in the presentation of his main points: the mark of the beast, one world government, wars and rumors of wars, widespread disease and famine. All of these pictures once again began to flash through my mind as I sat in the darkness minute after minute as the deafening roar of a nuclear blast continued for what seemed like an eternity. As the lights faded softly back on, I could see a multitude of others had made their way to the front of the auditorium to get their life right with Christ along with myself. I thought to myself over and over again "There is nothing in this world worth missing the rapture over!" That night was well over 20 years ago, and I am still as convinced as ever "There is nothing in this world worth missing the second coming of Christ for!" But as I age, I have found out the motivation is no longer fear, but love. I have fallen in love with the God of my salvation and some day, maybe sooner than any of us think, the trumpet of God will sound, the eastern sky shall part, and we who are alive in Christ shall be caught up to meet Him in the air.

We live in the last days before the Lords second coming. The vast majority of the ingredients are in place for Him to return. Are you ready to meet Him? Jesus said in Matthew 25:13; "Watch therefore, for you know neither the day nor the hour in which the Son of Man is coming" (NKJV). It's no longer popular for preachers to use the end time message to win converts to the Lord or to encourage people to get right, but the message, none the less, is still true?

He is coming?

Are you ready?

Application

End Times

1. Have a time of family prayer and devotion.
2. Is the second coming of Christ something we should be afraid of or look forward to with excitement?
3. What are your feelings about it?
4. On a scale of 1 –10: 1= not going, 10 = for sure going. What number would you say you are right now?
   - What is your biggest hindrance from being a 10?
   - Is that thing worth missing the rapture for?

5. Have a time of family prayer:
   - Start with thanksgiving and praise.
   - Repentance
   - Ask God to help you put everything in your life in proper perspective.
   - Pray for those in your world who do not know God or who have turned away from Him.
   - Pray God would help direct you to speak to them about God's love and His second coming.
   - Thank God for hearing your prayers.

Family Activity

Dessert Night

- Prepare cookies or brownies as a family.
- Make sure everyone has a part in the preparation.
- Make it as fun as possible.
- Enjoy the dessert together.

Everyone participating in the process and enjoying the results of the labor is in a way like heaven. By everyone doing their part, making it there together will make it all the more exciting and enjoyable!

Last Days

Scripture

Take turns reading the following scriptures out loud.

Acts 2:16-21; [16]But this is that which was spoken by the prophet Joel; [17]And it shall come to pass in the last days, saith God, I will pour out of my Spirit upon all flesh: and your sons and your daughters shall prophesy, and your young men shall see visions, and your old men shall dream dreams: [18]And on my servants and on my handmaidens I will pour out in those days of my Spirit; and they shall prophesy: [19]And I will shew wonders in heaven above, and signs in the earth beneath; blood, and fire, and vapour of smoke: [20]The sun shall be turned into darkness, and the moon into blood, before that great and notable day of the Lord come: [21]And it shall come to pass, that whosoever shall call on the name of the Lord shall be saved. KJV

2 Timothy 3:1-5; [1]You should know this, Timothy, that in the last days there will be very difficult times. [2]For people will love only themselves and their money. They will be boastful and proud, scoffing at God, disobedient to their parents, and ungrateful. They will consider nothing sacred. [3]They will be unloving and unforgiving; they will slander others and have no self-control. They will be cruel and hate what is good. [4]They will betray their friends, be reckless, be puffed up with pride, and love pleasure rather than God. [5]They will act religious, but they will reject the power that could make them godly. Stay away from people like that! NLT

Story: Jesus is Coming Soon

Are we living in the last days? This question has probably been asked over and over by every generation from the time of Jesus Christ's ascension. I remember hearing pastors and evangelists making the statement that we are in the last days and using the tragic events of the day to support their claim for the soon coming of the Lord. Famine, earthquakes, wars, and rumors of wars in various parts of the world all of these are predictors of the second coming of the Lord. There have been numerous groups of people that have sold all they had, quit their jobs, and went to mountain tops or rural places to prepare for the second coming only to be left sitting for days or weeks until they gave up. According to the prophet Joel, "And it shall come to pass in the last days, saith God, I will pour out of my Spirit upon all flesh." The last days were to begin with the initial outpouring of the Holy Spirit upon the believers, which was written about in Acts chapter 2. According to

this we have been in the last days for over 2000 years. So now men say we are in the last of the last days. Are we? Did the Christian world feel the same way during World War I or World War II? How about when Israel was surrounded on all sides by their enemy and thrown into a massive war in 1967? The massive earthquakes and tsunamis that killed thousands and rocked nations have men asking once again the question, "When?" There have been incidents all throughout history that led men to believe they were in the last of the last days and Christ's return would take place soon.

Jesus himself said in Matthew 25:13, "So you, too, must keep watch! For you do not know the day or hour of my return." So the important question is not "When is Jesus coming back?" but instead, "Am I faithful in doing His work?" Am I making sure my personal salvation is maintained? Am I witnessing to others and sharing the plan of salvation?

 **Application**

Last Days

1. Have a time of family prayer and devotion.
2. Have you been more concerned about when He will come back or more concerned about being involved in the work of His kingdom?
3. Do you feel secure with your own personal salvation?
4. Name two people in your life that need to hear the Good News of Jesus Christ? (death, burial, & resurrection)
5. What can you do to let them know about it?
   - Have a time of family prayer:
   - Start with thanksgiving and praise
   - Repentance
   - Ask God to help you have boldness in communicating the Gospel.
   - Pray for the two people you listed above, and that God would help provide an opportunity to speak to them.
   - Thank God for hearing your prayers.

 Family Activity

Connect with Two

Make contact with the two people on your list right now. (Don't wait until tomorrow. What if God comes back tonight?)
   - Call them and invite them to church or lunch.
   - Text them and let them know you are praying for them.
   - Send them a card of encouragement.
   - Communicate with them in a way that lets them know you were thinking about them and you have been praying for them.

Being friendly is the best way to introduce them to your best friend, Jesus!

Pray for these two people throughout the week.

Oneness of God

 ## Scripture

Take turns reading the following scriptures out loud.

Deuteronomy 6:4-7; ⁴ Hear, O Israel: The LORD our God is one LORD: ⁵ And thou shalt love the LORD thy God with all thine heart, and with all thy soul, and with all thy might. ⁶ And these words, which I command thee this day, shall be in thine heart: ⁷ And thou shalt teach them diligently unto thy children, and shalt talk of them when thou sittest in thine house, and when thou walkest by the way, and when thou liest down, and when thou risest up. KJV

1 Timothy 3:16; And without controversy great is the mystery of godliness: God was manifest in the flesh, justified in the Spirit, seen of angels, preached unto the Gentiles, believed on in the world, received up into glory. KJV

Story: The Lord Our God Is One

There is one God, and Jesus is His name! The Hebrew people of the Old Testament were surrounded by cultures who worshiped a multitude of Gods. Gods of the sun, moon, stars, rivers, and oceans, just about anything someone could think of that was mysterious or powerful was turned into a god to be worshiped. Some groups of people had literally hundreds of gods they worshiped. The Hebrew people held on to a very strict belief in one true God. When someone has a piece of truth that is very valuable, they make every attempt to make sure that those close to them also know that same precious truth. Deuteronomy 6:4 "Hear, O Israel! The Lord is our God, the Lord is one!" Fathers and mothers were directed to teach this truth to their children constantly. When they were sitting around at home, on a walk, or laying them down for bed at night, parents had the responsibility of instilling this precious truth. Mothers and fathers were given strict instructions to instill this truth in such a way that their children would always remember there is one true God.

It is important for us to understand and grasp the same revelation that the Hebrew people had way back then. There is only one God! God himself spoke to Isaiah and told him, "I am the first and the last; beside me there is no God." Over hundreds of years, people have changed the concept of whom and what God is to fit their own personal beliefs. Would it be possible to make a full grown wild tiger tame and cuddly like a house cat? No way!

They may both be from the same animal family, but their nature is completely different. It would be foolish to call a full grown wild tiger a little kitty just because that's what you want it to be. The same is true with God. He is who He is. It's not up to us to define Him, control Him, or manipulate Him. Is it even possible for men to change who God is? Hebrews 13:8-9 "Jesus Christ is the same yesterday, today, and forever. 9 Do not be carried about with various and strange doctrines." This scripture tells us God does not change. He never has changed and never will change. This scripture even warns us that people would try to twist and change the revelation of who and what God is to fit their own definitions of what they want God to be. While the majority of the Christian world considers the concept of the Trinity vital to Christianity, many historians and Bible scholars agree that the Trinity of Christianity owes more to Greek philosophy and pagan polytheism than to the monotheism of the Jew and the Jewish Jesus.

So what happened? How did the vast majority of Christianity move from the foundation of one God? They neglected to follow through on one simple action prescribed in the Old Testament Deuteronomy 6:7 states "You shall teach them diligently to your sons and shall talk of them when you sit in your house and when you walk by the way and when you lie down and when you rise up."

My concern is not whether God is on our side; my great concern is to be on God's side, for God is always right.

 <u>**Application**</u>

Oneness of God

1. Have a time of family prayer and devotion:
   - Praise and worship God.
   - Repentance
2. Pray for each family member one at a time.
   - Have them name one prayer request for themselves and one for someone else.
   - Lay hands on them while you pray for their requests.
3. Pray that God would help your family hold on to the vital truth of One True God.

 <u>**Family Activity**</u>

Scripture Memory

Look up a few key scriptures that emphasize the truth of who God is:
- Deuteronomy 6:4
- Revelation 1:8
- Malachi 3:6
- Isaiah 44:6
- Psalm 86:10

Choose one or two scriptures to write on a 3x5 card and commit to memorize it. Quote it to one another when you wake up in the morning, before dinner, and when you lie down for bed.

Seek and You Will Find

 Scripture
Take turns reading the following scriptures out loud.

Luke 11:10; For everyone who asks, receives; and he who seeks, finds; and to him who knocks, it will be opened. NASB

Isaiah 55:6-9; [6]Seek the Lord while He may be found; Call upon Him while He is near. [7]Let the wicked forsake his way And the unrighteous man his thoughts; And let him return to the Lord, And He will have compassion on him, And to our God, For He will abundantly pardon. [8]For My thoughts are not your thoughts, Nor are your ways My ways, declares the Lord. [9]For as the heavens are higher than the earth, So are My ways higher than your ways And My thoughts than your thoughts. NASB

Story: Where Are You?

We were on our annual Christmas trek to Chicago. Each year we brought our family to spend time with Grandpa and Grandma and visit the museums. This year we decided to finish our Christmas shopping at suburban Woodfield Mall. In the midst of all the fun and excitement, one of us noticed that little 3 1/2 year-old Matthew was gone. Terror immediately struck our hearts. We had heard the horror stories: little children kidnapped in malls, rushed to a restroom, donned in different clothes and altered hairstyle, and then swiftly smuggled out, never to be seen again. We split up, each taking an assigned location. Mine was the parking lot. I'll never forget that night kicking through the newly fallen snow, calling out his name at the top of my lungs. I felt so foolish yelling at the top of my lungs, but my concern for Matthew's safety outweighed all other feelings.

Unsuccessful, I trudged back to our meeting point. My wife, Martie, had not found him, nor had my mother. And then my dad appeared, holding little Matthew by the hand. Our hearts leapt for joy. Interestingly enough, Matthew was untraumatized. He hadn't been crying. To him,

there had been no problem. I asked my father where he had found him. "The candy counter," he replied. "You should have seen him. His eyes came just about as high as the candy. He held his little hands behind his back and moved his head back and forth, surveying all the luscious options." Matthew didn't look lost. He didn't know he was lost. He was oblivious to the phenomenal danger he was in. Today's society is a candy-counter culture, where people who don't look lost and don't know they're lost live for the consumption of their every desire.

It's intriguing that the Lord never loses sight of us, but we often lose sight of Him. He never takes His ever watchful eyes off of us, and He is concerned about our every need. We on the other hand, get caught up in the attractive displays of this world that draw our attention off of God, just like the candy drew the attention of the lost little boy away from his protectors. We too don't realize we are lost until it's too late, and we have lost sight of God. The reassuring thing is He is always just as close as a prayer of repentance and the mention of His name, Jesus!

Ref.: Joseph M. Stowell, *Moody Monthly*, December, 1989, p. 4.

Seek and You Will Find

1. Have a time of family prayer and devotion.
   - Talk about a time you or someone you know was lost.
   - Were you scared?
   - What did you do?
2. How did everything turn out?
3. The U.S. Department of Justice report for 2002, states that 797,500 children (younger than 18) were reported missing in a one-year period of time studied resulting in an average of 2,185 children being reported missing each day.
4. How many more people do you think lose sight of God?
5. What does seeking the Lord mean to you?
   - Have a time of family prayer:
   - Start with thanksgiving and praise.
   - Repentance
   - Take turns praying for each family member:
     - They would turn their focus back to God.
     - Pray for children that the blood of Jesus would cover them.
     - Pray that family members would never be lost in their relationship with God.
   - Thank God for hearing your prayers.

 __Family Activity__

Hide-n-Seek

- Designate one place in the house to be base (the safe spot)
- Turn off most of the light in the house except for the lights near the base.
- The person who is it must count slowly to 20 while everyone hides.
- The first person tagged is it the next time.
- You can take turns being it to ensure everyone gets a chance.

Serving My Family

Scripture

Take turns reading the following scriptures out loud.

John 13: 1-5, 12-17; [1]Before the Passover celebration, Jesus knew that his hour had come to leave this world and return to his Father. He had loved his disciples during his ministry on earth, and now he loved them to the very end. [2]It was time for supper, and the devil had already prompted Judas, son of Simon Iscariot, to betray Jesus. [3]Jesus knew that the Father had given him authority over everything and that he had come from God and would return to God. [4]So he got up from the table, took off his robe, wrapped a towel around his waist, [5]and poured water into a basin. Then he began to wash the disciples' feet, drying them with the towel he had around him

[12]After washing their feet, he put on his robe again and sat down and asked, "Do you understand what I was doing? [13]You call me 'Teacher' and 'Lord,' and you are right, because that's what I am. [14]And since I, your Lord and Teacher, have washed your feet, you ought to wash each other's feet. [15]I have given you an example to follow. Do as I have done to you. [16]I tell you the truth, slaves are not greater than their master. Nor is the messenger more important than the one who sends the message. [17]Now that you know these things, God will bless you for doing them." NLT

Story: Jesus Served

The practice of foot washing appears to be found in the hospitality customs of ancient civilizations. Sandals were the primary foot wear for the vast majority of people in the Middle East region where Israel is located and people's feet would get dusty and dirty as they journeyed from one place to another. Therefore, a host would provide water for guests to wash their feet, provide a servant to wash the feet of the guests, or even serve the guests by washing their feet themselves. The first time we read of foot washing is when Abraham or his servant washes the feet of three visitors, who were really angels of the Lord. Foot washing was something the servant typically did for someone who was an honored guest. It was done as a sign to the guest to let them know they were important and valuable to the person whose home they visited.

In our scriptures we see Jesus, who is the King of Kings and Lord of Lords, taking the position of a servant and washing the feet of all of His disciples. What would cause Jesus to do such a thing? John 13:3; Jesus knew that the Father had given him authority over everything and that he had come from God and would return to God. The knowledge that He had all power and authority caused Him to act and He wanted to set for His disciples an example for them to follow. 4 So he got up from the table, took off his robe, wrapped a towel around his waist. Faith in God's Word and faith in His promises should cause us to act as Jesus did. We should serve because we love, because we care, and because we are not concerned about position or authority. We are to follow the example set by Jesus that night and serve because we have been told by Jesus we ought to serve. John 13:12-15; "Do you understand what I was doing? 13 You call me 'Teacher' and 'Lord,' and you are right, because that's what I am. 14 And since I, your Lord and Teacher, have washed your feet, you ought to wash each other's feet. 15 I have given you an example to follow. Do as I have done to you." A job traditionally designated for a servant, was completed by the Master to teach His disciples that in His kingdom, the greatest among us shall be servant to all out of love.

Who are the ones we should serve the most? Who do we have the greatest impact upon on a daily basis? Where does my Christ-like attitude need to be on its greatest display? With our family, at home, is the obvious answer. Are you serving like Jesus?

 **Application**

Serving My Family

1. Prepare for a time of family prayer and foot washing.
2. First have a time of individual prayer:
   - Praise and worship God.
   - Repentance
   - Ask God to help you serve each other just like Jesus served His disciples.
3. Wash each other's feet.
   - The head of the house should start first by washing the feet of the youngest.
   - The rest of the family should gather around, lay hands on the one whose feet are being washed and on the one who is washing, and pray with them and for them.
   - Several family members can wash someone's feet at the same time to expedite the process.
   - The goal is that everyone in the house has taken the position of a servant to the other family members.
   - Take turns until everyone has washed each other's feet.
4. Gather together for a time of family prayer to conclude your time together.

 **Family Activity**

Game Time

Pull out a game that gets everyone involved but requires one person to be in charge. Example: Cards, Monopoly, Life. These games have one person that deals all the cards to everyone else or has a banker who is in charge of all the money. Talk about how it appears that one person has all the power, but in reality that person is there to serve all the others and make the game work. Without that person serving others the game could not be played.

Baptism of Water and Spirit

Scripture

Take turns reading the following scriptures out loud.

John 3:1-5; [1]There was a man of the Pharisees, named Nicodemus, a ruler of the Jews: [2]The same came to Jesus by night, and said unto him, Rabbi, we know that thou art a teacher come from God: for no man can do these miracles that thou doest, except God be with him. [3]Jesus answered and said unto him, Verily, verily, I say unto thee, Except a man be born again, he cannot see the kingdom of God. [4]Nicodemus saith unto him, How can a man be born when he is old? Can he enter the second time into his mother's womb, and be born? [5]Jesus answered, Verily, verily, I say unto thee, Except a man be born of water and of the Spirit, he cannot enter into the kingdom of God. KJV

Story: Born Again

Night had fallen in Jerusalem. A crowd of religious teachers had gathered to discuss the strange teachings of an uneducated carpenter named Jesus. "Who does he think he is?" said one man, "He has never even been to our schools of religious instruction." "I heard someone say he is just the son of a carpenter," said another man. A young man at the back of the crowd spoke up, "We cannot argue with the fact that he does many miracles, signs, and wonders. I wonder if he is the one we have been waiting for?" An instantaneous roar of arguing erupted within the gathering of the religious teachers and leaders. As the arguing raged on, Nicodemus slips out of the temple into the cold, dark moonlit street. Nicodemus had heard the teaching of this man named Jesus and even seen the miracles that had taken place with his own eyes.

Nicodemus' mind wandered back to the temple courtyard two days ago when Jesus drove out the moneychangers with a whip. The moneychangers had always bothered Nicodemus and he secretly smiled with delight to see someone with enough zeal and passion for the house of God stand up and drive those crooks out. He turned the corner and headed down the dusty street towards home. A cold breeze rose out of the valley and into his face causing him to pull his outer cloak tighter around his neck and chest. Off in the distance he could see a group of men gathered around a fire. As he got closer he could clearly see the outline of the man Jesus. His heart raced with excitement and fear. He wanted desperately to talk to Him and now was his chance, in the dark of the night where none of the religious rulers or teachers would see him talking to Jesus. As Nicodemus walked into the light of the small fire,

he noticed that Jesus was already rising from his seat and looking directly into his eyes. His nerves raced as the twelve men sitting around the fire stared at him. Nicodemus knew his time with Jesus would be brief. He would only have a few minutes to ask Jesus for the answer to the question that was nagging at his soul. It was now or never. The crackle of the fire and a dog barking off in the distance were the only sounds that broke the silence. Nicodemus cleared his dry throat and spoke, "Rabbi, we know that thou art a teacher come from God: for no man can do these miracles that thou doest, except God be with him." 3 Jesus answered and said unto him, "Verily, verily, I say unto thee, Except a man be born again, he cannot see the kingdom of God."

Jesus does not even bother to respond to Nicodemus' statement, but instead addresses the true question that has troubled Nicodemus' soul. What must I do to be saved? 4 Nicodemus saith unto him, "How can a man be born when he is old? Can he enter the second time into his mother's womb, and be born?" 5 Jesus answered, "Verily, verily, I say unto thee, Except a man be born of water and of the Spirit, he cannot enter into the kingdom of God." The encounter was brief, but the words spoken by Jesus answered the question that was gnawing at the soul of Nicodemus. 2000 years later the same question burns in the hearts of men and women and the answer is still the same. You must be born again of water and Spirit to enter the kingdom of God. Good works, a sinner's prayer, praying the rosary, or other forms of religious practice will never replace the one and only method of joining the kingdom of God, Baptism of Water and of the Spirit!

 ## Application

Baptism of Water and Spirit

1. Have a time of family prayer and devotion:
   - Praise and worship God.
   - Repentance
2. Have you been born again of the water and Spirit as instructed by Jesus in John 3:5?
3. Do you know someone who has not been born again of the water and the Spirit?
   - Pray for them tonight and the remainder of the week.
4. Pray for each family member one at a time.
   - Have them name one prayer request for themselves and one for someone else.
   - Lay hands on them while you pray for their requests.

 ## Family Activity

Sword Drill

Have one person call out a scripture. The first person to find the scripture, stand up, and start reading it out loud gets a point.

Recommended Scriptures:
- John 3:5
- Acts 2:38
- Acts 1:5
- Acts 2:4
- Isaiah 28:11
- Mark 16:17
- Hebrews 6:1-2
- Acts 4:12

Jesus Name Baptism

 Scripture

Take turns reading the following scriptures out loud.

Matthew 28: 18-20; [18]And Jesus came and spake unto them, saying, All power is given unto me in heaven and in earth. [19]Go ye therefore, and teach all nations, baptizing them in the name of the Father, and of the Son, and of the Holy Ghost: [20]Teaching them to observe all things whatsoever I have commanded you: and, lo, I am with you alway, even unto the end of the world. Amen. KJV

Acts 2:38-39; [38]Then Peter said unto them, Repent, and be baptized every one of you in the name of Jesus Christ for the remission of sins, and ye shall receive the gift of the Holy Ghost. [39]For the promise is unto you, and to your children, and to all that are afar off, even as many as the Lord our God shall call. KJV

Story: No Other Name

The resurrected Lord sat and spoke with His beloved disciples. Eleven of them were left, as the position of Judas had not yet been filled. The time Jesus had with the remaining eleven disciples was valuable and short. He needed to instill in them as much as possible over the next few days. He reminded them of many things He had spoke of during the three years while they walked around the area of Judea from one town to the next. As He connected the dots of previous teachings and events that had transpired during His persecution and eventual crucifixion, revelation began to flood the minds of the apostles. As precious valuable time ticked on, Jesus knew He would have to ascend into the heavens and He would no longer physically be able to be with his disciples and provide them verbal and physical instruction. He must go away so He could send the comforter, the Spirit, to be with them always. Matthew records the conversation as follows: "Jesus spoke unto them, saying, All power is given unto me in heaven and in earth. 19 Go ye therefore, and teach all nations, baptizing them in the name of the Father, and of the Son, and of the Holy Ghost: 20 Teaching them to observe all things whatsoever I have commanded you: and, lo, I am with you always, even unto the end of the world." After Jesus ascends into the heavens the disciples and numerous others go to Jerusalem and await the promise of the Holy Spirit as Jesus had told them to do. Acts chapter two records the wondrous event of that Spiritual infilling of God's Spirit into the heart and soul of mankind. Truly God would no longer live in a man-made temple but would now inhabit the soul of mankind and have divine relationship with him.

Peter and the other eleven disciples stand up to address the crowd that has gathered. Acts 2:38; "Then Peter said unto them, Repent, and be baptized every one of you in the name of Jesus Christ for the remission of sins, and ye shall receive the gift of the Holy Ghost." Had Peter made a mistake? Did he mess up the first message preached after the initial outpouring of the Holy Spirit by saying that everyone must be baptized in the name of Jesus Christ instead of what Jesus himself said in Matthew 28:19? Why didn't one of the other eleven disciples correct this mistake? Because it was no mistake at all! All eleven disciples knew from the teaching of Jesus himself that the name of the Father is Jesus, the name of the Son is Jesus, and the name of the Holy Spirit is Jesus. There was no mistake; there is no contradiction in scripture or in the teaching of Jesus himself. Peter himself is recorded again two chapters later in Acts 2:12 before the religious rulers of the day as saying, "Neither is there salvation in any other: for there is none other name under heaven given among men, whereby we must be saved." The saving name is Jesus! The name of the Father, Son, and Holy Ghost is Jesus.

 **Application**

Jesus Name Baptism

1. Have a time of family prayer and devotion:
   - Start with praise and worship unto God.
   - Repentance
2. Go to the bedroom of the youngest family member and pray for them there.
   - Be very specific praying for them by name.
   - Have them share one personal request and one prayer request for someone outside of the family.
3. Finish your prayer time in the living room by thanking God for hearing and answering your prayers.

 Family Activity

Impostor
(A version of charades where you try to act like someone else)

- Have one person pretend to be someone everyone knows.
- The person acting cannot say any words except the words yes or no.
- For young children allow them to say words to help them impersonate the person they chose.

The person who correctly guesses the name of the impostor will go next.
The titles dad, mom, brother, sister, grandma and grandpa are shared by billions of people worldwide. The value and identity of a person is wrapped up in their name. Our God, our Savior, our Redeemer has a name: Jesus. Love that name!

Persecution

Scripture

Take turns reading the following scriptures out loud.

Leviticus 26:1; "You shall not make idols for yourselves; neither a carved image nor a sacred pillar shall you rear up for yourselves; nor shall you set up an engraved stone in your land, to bow down to it; for I am the Lord your God." NKJV

Daniel 3:1-15; ¹King Nebuchadnezzar made a gold statue ninety feet tall and nine feet wide and set it up on the plain of Dura in the province of Babylon. ²Then he sent messages to the high officers, officials, governors, advisers, treasurers, judges, magistrates, and all the provincial officials to come to the dedication of the statue he had set up. ³So all these officials came and stood before the statue King Nebuchadnezzar had set up.

⁴Then a herald shouted out, "People of all races and nations and languages, listen to the king's command! ⁵When you hear the sound of the horn, flute, zither, lyre, harp, pipes, and other musical instruments, bow to the ground to worship King Nebuchadnezzar's gold statue. ⁶Anyone who refuses to obey will immediately be thrown into a blazing furnace."

⁷So at the sound of the musical instruments, all the people, whatever their race or nation or language, bowed to the ground and worshiped the gold statue that King Nebuchadnezzar had set up.

⁸But some of the astrologers went to the king and informed on the Jews. ⁹They said to King Nebuchadnezzar, "Long live the king! ¹⁰You issued a decree requiring all the people to bow down and worship the gold statue when they hear the sound of the horn, flute, zither, lyre, harp, pipes, and other musical instruments. ¹¹That decree also states that those who refuse to obey must be thrown into a blazing furnace. ¹²But there are some Jews—Shadrach, Meshach, and Abednego—whom you have put in charge of the province of Babylon. They pay no attention to you, Your Majesty. They refuse to serve your gods and do not worship the gold statue you have set up."

¹³Then Nebuchadnezzar flew into a rage and ordered that Shadrach, Meshach, and Abednego be brought before him. When they were brought in, ¹⁴Nebuchadnezzar said to them, "Is it true, Shadrach, Meshach, and Abednego, that you refuse to serve my gods or to worship the gold statue I have set up? ¹⁵I will give you one more chance to bow down and worship the statue I have made when you hear the sound of the musical instruments. But if you refuse, you will be thrown immediately into the blazing furnace. And then what god will be able to rescue you from my power?" NLT

Story: Free to Worship

Talk about pressure! The three Hebrew boys were facing what appears to be a life or death situation. Fall to your knees and worship an idol or be cast into the fire. Most of us today have never been forced into a situation where we had to make a decision like the one presented to the three Hebrew boys that day. In America we enjoy a whole host of freedoms that allow us to worship the one true God freely without threat of persecution by the government. Most of us will never know what it is like to have a gun pointed at us and told that if we worship God or pray to Him we will be killed. Yet there are people all over the world who face such persecution on a regular basis. Our fellow Christian believers who are part of the underground church in China, Pakistan, North Korea, and a host of other African and Muslim countries, face the possibility of death every time they open their Bibles or gather for a church service. Even with the possibility of death, these believers have developed such a love for God and His Word that they are willing to lose their lives to worship and praise the Lord Jesus Christ.

Persecution

1. Discuss the following questions before having your family prayer time:
    - Would it be difficult for you to live in one of the countries listed above in the story and still serve God?
    - How do you think Christians in these countries maintain their relationship with God as they face the real possibility of death just by attending a church service?
    - How did persecution affect the early church in the book of Acts?
    - Do Christians in America struggle with their commitment to God because we have it so easy and don't have to worry about persecution?
    - Will Americans someday lose the freedom to worship God freely?
    - Do you face persecution on any level for what you believe?

2. Have a time of family prayer and devotion
    - Start with praise and worship unto God.
    - Repentance

3. Pray for missionaries and believers in other countries that face the possibility of persecution for worshiping God.

4. If you have a map or a globe, use it to choose one country to focus on and ask God to bless and empower the Christian missionaries and believers of that country.

Sign of the Holy Spirit

Scripture

Take turns reading the following scriptures out loud.

Acts 2:1-4; [1]When the day of Pentecost had come, they were all together in one place. [2]And suddenly there came from heaven a noise like a violent rushing wind, and it filled the whole house where they were sitting. [3]And there appeared to them tongues as of fire distributing themselves, and they rested on each one of them. [4]And they were all filled with the Holy Spirit and began to speak with other tongues, as the Spirit was giving them utterance. NASB

Acts 2:38-39; [38]Then Peter said unto them, Repent, and be baptized every one of you in the name of Jesus Christ for the remission of sins, and ye shall receive the gift of the Holy Ghost. [39]For the promise is unto you, and to your children, and to all that are afar off, even as many as the Lord our God shall call. KJV

Story: The Day of Pentecost

We read in the second chapter of Acts that when the Holy Spirit was poured out upon the 120 believers who had gathered together in the upper room that they spoke in another tongue. Speaking in tongues is "the supernatural gift of speaking in another language without having learned that language." God is the giver of this miraculous gift. Speaking in tongues is the sign that God's Spirit is in us and upon us in a powerful way. The prophet Isaiah foretold of the gift God would pour out on His people in the 28th chapter. "For with stammering lips and another tongue will he speak to this people. To whom he said, This is the rest wherewith ye may cause the weary to rest; and this is the refreshing." God chose the most uncontrollable part of our body to hold or display the sign we had surrendered our life completely to Him, and that part of our body is our tongue. James 3:8 says, "But the tongue can no man tame; it is an unruly evil, full of deadly poison." God, by His power, moves upon us and uses our tongue and our spirit to glorify and praise Him. What a strange and magnificent way for God to show His power and love!

It's no wonder that on the day of Pentecost when the Spirit of God filled the 120 believers, there was a great crowd of people that gathered around to see what was happening. 120 people speaking in a language they were not taught! There were Jewish people, born and raised right around Jerusalem, speaking in languages from all around the world. The people who had come from distant lands to participate in the celebration of Pentecost heard Jews speaking perfectly in the language of their far away country. Before the day ended, over 3000 people were added to the church because they heard and saw fellow Jews speaking in tongues and glorifying God.

The outpouring of the Holy Spirit upon people still attracts the attention of people today. Not only do people feel a tremendous rush of peace, power, love, grace, acceptance, and relief from the burdens of life when they are filled with God's Spirit, but they are provided with a sign for themselves and everyone around them that they have been filled with God's Spirit. Paul said it best when speaking to the fellow believers in Corinth, "Have you received the Holy Ghost since you believed?" The gift is still for you and me today. It's not just a one time experience, but something we can experience day after day, week after week.

Sign of the Holy Spirit

1. Have a time of family prayer and devotion:
   - Start with praise and worship unto God.
   - Repentance (Parents walk your children through this step so they know exactly what to do.)

2. Read Acts 19:1-6;
   - Ask everyone in your family devotion the same question Paul asked the Corinthians, "Have you received since you believed?"
   - Pray for a fresh renewal of God's Spirit in each and every member of your family devotion.

3. Have each person in the devotion pray for one person who needs to receive the Spirit of God into their life.
   - Pray for one personal need at the same time.
   - Create faith! Yes, God is still filling people with His Spirit in people's homes all the time.

 **Family Activity**

Family Walk in the Park

Choose a nice park or a remote scenic location where you live to take the family on a nature walk. If these two options are too far away, just take a nice walk around the block.

Notice how every living thing makes a sound. Birds chirp, dogs bark, cats meow, and people talk. Sounds are all around us. Even many insects make a sound when they are busy at their work. The Spirit of God also makes a sound when He fills the hearts and souls of believers. It is the sound of speaking in tongues! Let God move through you this week. Pray in the Spirit as much as you can!

Societal Pressure

Scripture
Take turns reading the following scriptures out loud.

2 Corinthians 6:17-18; [17]Therefore come out from among them, and be ye separate, saith the Lord, and touch not the unclean thing; and I will receive you, [18]And will be a Father unto you, and ye shall be my sons and daughters, saith the Lord Almighty. KJV

2 Corinthians 6:14-18; [14]Don't team up with those who are unbelievers. How can righteousness be a partner with wickedness? How can light live with darkness? [15]What harmony can there be between Christ and the devil? How can a believer be a partner with an unbeliever? [16]And what union can there be between God's temple and idols? For we are the temple of the living God. As God said; "I will live in them and walk among them. I will be their God, and they will be my people. [17]Therefore, come out from among unbelievers, and separate yourselves from them, says the Lord. Don't touch their filthy things, and I will welcome you. [18]And I will be your Father, and you will be my sons and daughters, says the Lord Almighty." NLT

Story: Peer Pressure

Once a spider built a beautiful web in an old house, he kept it clean and shiny so flies would patronize it. The minute he got a "customer" he would clean him up so the other flies would not get suspicious. Then one day, this fairly intelligent fly came buzzing by the clean spider web. Old man spider called out, "Come in and sit," but the fairly intelligent fly said, "No, sir. I don't see other flies in your house, and I am not going in alone!"

At the same time he saw on the floor below a large crowd of flies dancing around on a piece of yellow paper. He was delighted! He was not afraid if lots of flies were doing it. So he came in for a landing. Just before he landed, a bee zoomed by, saying, "Don't land there, dummy! That's flypaper!" But the fairly intelligent fly shouted back, "Don't be silly. Those flies are dancing. There's a big crowd there. Everybody's doing it. That many flies can't be wrong!"

Well, you know what happened. He landed in the middle of all those other flies and was instantly stuck just like them. He died on the spot. Some of us want to be with the crowd so badly we end up in a mess. What does it profit a fly (or a person) if he escapes the web only to end up in the glue?

There is a lot of pressure to be just like everyone else. As long as man has walked this earth, he has felt the pressure to do the same things, act the same way, dress like, and talk like the other people around them. Adam ate the forbidden fruit because Eve did. The people of Israel worshiped God's made of wood and stone because their neighbors did. Peter denied he even knew the Lord Jesus three times because he could not stand against the pressure of those who were putting the Lord on trial. Just because someone around you is doing something does not mean it is right. The pressure to do what others are doing is a natural emotion you will have to battle with all of your life. You must learn early in life that you have to follow the direction and guidance of people that love and serve God with all of their hearts, strength, and mind. Why don't you start creating your own peer pressure; worship God, serve God, love God and love His people with all of your might. Make those around you feel pressure to do what is right. That's the kind of peer pressure we need in the church and amongst God's people.

 ## Application

Societal Pressure

1. Have a time of family prayer and devotion:
   - Start with praise and worship unto God.
   - Repentance

2. Tell of a time in your life when following the crowd got you into trouble.

3. Tell of a time in your life when following the crowd was a good thing in your life.
   - Worship in church, helping someone in need, community service projects, etc.

4. Pray for people that you know who are not making right choices.
   - Pray God would help you be a positive influence in their life.

5. Pray God would help you do what is right when you are faced with the pressure to go along with the crowd.

 ## Family Activity

Follow the Leader

Take turns and go from youngest to oldest and play follow the leader. Give the leader about 3 to 5 minutes to go wherever they want. Make it difficult and try to go through places that everyone else may not be able to go through.

Once the adults get their turn change the game to include:
- Reading passages from the Bible. Give the scripture and wait until everyone finds it in their Bible, read the scripture out loud together.
- Worship God! Someone lead the family in praise and worship unto our God.

Asking for Forgiveness

Scripture

Take turns reading the following scriptures out loud.

Psalm 65: 3-4; [3]Though we are overwhelmed by our sins, you forgive them all.4 What joy for those you choose to bring near, those who live in your holy courts. What festivities await us inside your holy Temple. NLT

Psalm 103:2-5; [2]Let all that I am praise the Lord; may I never forget the good things he does for me. [3]He forgives all my sins and heals all my diseases. [4]He redeems me from death and crowns me with love and tender mercies. [5]He fills my life with good things. My youth is renewed like the eagle's! NLT

1 John 1:8-9; [8]If we claim we have no sin, we are only fooling ourselves and not living in the truth. [9]But if we confess our sins to him, he is faithful and just to forgive us our sins and to cleanse us from all wickedness. NLT

Story: A Dead Duck

A little boy visiting his grandparents during summer vacation was given his first slingshot. He practiced in the woods all day long, but could never hit his target. As he came back to Grandma's backyard, he spied her pet duck off over by the pond. On an impulse, he took aim and let a rock fly towards the duck. To his amazement the rock hit the duck and it fell dead.

Shocked and stunned the boy panicked. He ran over to the poor little duck and tried to revive it. When he realized he had killed his Grandmother's pet duck he was scared he would be in big trouble, and so he hid the dead duck in the woodpile, only to look up and see his sister watching. His sister Sally had seen it all, but she said nothing. After lunch that day, Grandma said, "Sally, let's wash the dishes." But Sally looked up at Johnny and said, "Johnny told me he wanted to help in the kitchen today. Didn't you, Johnny?" And she whispered to him, "Remember the duck!" So Johnny did the dishes.

Later Grandpa asked if the children wanted to go fishing. Grandma said, "I'm sorry, but I need Sally to help make supper." Sally smiled and said, "That's all taken care of. Johnny wants to do it." Again she leaned over and whispered in Johnny's ear, "Remember the duck." Johnny stayed and helped grandma in the kitchen while Sally went fishing. After several days of Johnny doing both his chores and Sally's, finally he couldn't stand it anymore. He confessed to Grandma. "Grandma," Johnny said, "I have a confession I need to make to you. The other day when I was coming out of the woods I shot a rock at your duck and accidentally hit him. It was the only thing I hit all day! I'm really sorry Grandma, I know it was your favorite duck and I feel so bad. I killed your favorite duck." "I know, Johnny," said Grandma, giving him a hug. "I was standing at the window and saw the whole thing. Because I love you, I forgave you even before you asked. I wondered how long you would let Sally make a slave of you before you would confess your wrong action."

The failure to confess our wrong actions and ask for forgiveness has the ability to make a slave out of us. Guilt will cause a person to hide from people they love and from God. We become a slave to guilt and condemnation. Guilt can ruin our lives if we allow it to. A famous psychiatrist once said that if he could convince the patients in psychiatric hospitals their sins were forgiven, 75 percent of them could walk out the next day. What a powerful effect forgiveness can have on our lives. We inadvertently run from the love and grace of God and family members who only want what is best for us. The hard part is standing still, refusing to run from guilt and shame, and saying sorry to those we have either let down or done wrong too. The Bible says in 1 John "But if we confess our sins to him, he is faithful and just to forgive us our sins and to cleanse us from all wickedness." There is no need to carry around the heaviness of guilt when God is ready and willing to take the weight off of our backs and offer us forgiveness as soon as we ask.

Application

Asking for Forgiveness

1. If it was you in the story that had killed the duck would you have hid it in the wood pile also or would you have told your Grandma?

2. Has guilt ever kept you from having a good relationship with someone? Example: Parents, friends, God...

3. Have you ever had to lie to cover up something wrong that you did because you thought it would be easier to lie than tell the truth?

4. Have a time of family prayer and devotion:
   • Start with praise and worship.
   • Have a time of repentance.
   • Forgive anyone in your life that you may have bad feelings towards.
   • Ask God to forgive you of any wrongs.
   • Spend time praying for each other individually. Pray that God would help you realize the freedom that comes from asking for forgiveness and telling the truth. Pray for someone in your life that needs forgiveness.

Family Activity

Guilt Tag
(same as freeze tag)

Go outside into an open area (yard, school, park, etc.) One person will be the "Guilt". When the "Guilt" tags someone they have to freeze where they are tagged. The "Guilt" has frozen them and they are not supposed to move until another player touches and unfreezes them.

Once everyone is frozen with guilt, the last player tagged now becomes the "Guilt" and everyone else is free to run again!

Just like the power of forgiveness to us spiritually, the instant we are touched by God with forgiveness we are free from the "Guilt" and condemnation of sin. We are free to run once again!

Go eat some "Guilt-Free" ice cream when you are done playing!

Impress Them on Your Children

 Scripture

Take turns reading the following scriptures out loud.

Deuteronomy 6:1-9; [1]These are the commands, decrees and laws the Lord your God directed me to teach you to observe in the land that you are crossing the Jordan to possess, [2]so that you, your children and their children after them may fear the Lord your God as long as you live by keeping all his decrees and commands that I give you, and so that you may enjoy long life. [3]Hear, O Israel, and be careful to obey so that it may go well with you and that you may increase greatly in a land flowing with milk and honey, just as the Lord, the God of your fathers, promised you.

[4]Hear, O Israel: The Lord our God, the Lord is one. [5]Love the Lord your God with all your heart and with all your soul and with all your strength. [6]These commandments that I give you today are to be upon your hearts. [7]Impress them on your children. Talk about them when you sit at home and when you walk along the road, when you lie down and when you get up. [8]Tie them as symbols on your hands and bind them on your foreheads. [9]Write them on the doorframes of your houses and on your gates. NIV

Story: Actions Speak Louder than Words

Life is a matter of building. Each of us has the opportunity to build something—a secure family, a good reputation, a career, a relationship with God. However, some of those things can disappear almost overnight due to financial losses, natural disasters, and other unforeseen difficulties.

What are we to do? Daniel Webster offered excellent advice, saying, "If we work on marble it will perish. If we work on brass, time will efface it. If we build temples, they will crumble to dust. However; if we work on men's immortal minds, if we instill in them high principles, with just fear of God and love for their fellow-men, we engrave on those tablets something which time cannot destroy, and which will brighten and brighten to all eternity."

Many people ponder what items of value they can leave to the next generation when their time comes to pass from this life to the next. Money, gold, stocks and bonds, houses, land, and personal keepsakes that have been in the family for generations are all valuable items in the eyes of this world. How much of an impact do these items really have on the succeeding generations that receive them? A tremendous impact! Most remaining family member's who receive an inheritance fight, bicker, alienate one another and most often end up in worse financial shape than if they did not receive the inheritance at all.

What can a person do to make sure that they are leaving their children something of long lasting value in their lives? Moses writes in Deuteronomy that God directed him to teach Israel to observe the law in the promise land so that the succeeding generations can enjoy a long and prosperous life in the land. The respect and reverence of God was paramount in Israel's relationship with God and that reverence and respect towards God had to be passed down to the succeeding generations. Moses said to "Impress them on your children." Impress means to leave such an impact upon someone or something that it forever changes the item or individual in a favorable way. God's people, you and I, are directed to do everything we possibly can to impress our children with God's law and love that we are told to talk about them when we sit at home, when we drive along the road, when we lie down and when we get up. Tie them as symbols on your hands and bind them on your foreheads. Write them on the doorframes of your houses and on your gates. In other words, God is saying do whatever is necessary to make this impression! The more you talk about God and the benefits of serving God, the more you show those close to you the value of being faithful to the Savior the more impressed they become with the presence of God. Love the Lord your God with all your heart and with all your soul and with all your strength. Remember the impression of your actions goes much deeper and last much longer than your words.

 ## Application

Impress Them on Your Children

1. Have a time of family prayer and devotion:
   - Start with praise and worship.
   - Have a time of repentance.

2. Pray the following scripture: Psalm 119: 9-15

   [9] How can a young person stay pure? By obeying your word. [10] I have tried hard to find you—don't let me wander from your commands. [11] I have hidden your word in my heart, that I might not sin against you. [12] I praise you, O Lord; teach me your decrees. [13] I have recited aloud all the regulations you have given us. [14] I have rejoiced in your laws as much as in riches. [15] I will study your commandments and reflect on your ways. [16] I will delight in your decrees and not forget your word

3. Pray for individual and family needs together.

 ## Family Activity

Homemade Play-Dough

- 1 cup flour, 1 cup water
- 1 tablespoon oil, 1 tablespoon powdered alum
- 1/2 cup salt, 2 tablespoons vanilla, food coloring
- Mix all dry ingredients. Add oil and water. Cook over medium heat, stirring constantly until reaching the consistency of mashed potatoes. Remove from heat and add vanilla and food coloring. Divide into balls and work in color by kneading the playdough.

Sit down and spend time shaping and sculpting the dough. For the dough to take shape pressure must be applied to it. The same is true of your spirit. God wants us to have a heart that is shaped and molded by His Word. God places people in our lives that impress His Word and love into our lives to change us for the better.

Purpose of Proverbs

Scripture

Take turns reading the following scriptures out loud.

Proverbs 1:1-7; [1]These are the proverbs of Solomon, David's son, king of Israel. [2]Their purpose is to teach people wisdom and discipline, to help them understand the insights of the wise. [3]Their purpose is to teach people to live disciplined and successful lives, to help them do what is right, just, and fair. [4]These proverbs will give insight to the simple, knowledge and discernment to the young. [5]Let the wise listen to these proverbs and become even wiser. Let those with understanding receive guidance [6]by exploring the meaning in these proverbs and parables, the words of the wise and their riddles. [7]Fear of the Lord is the foundation of true knowledge, but fools despise wisdom and discipline. NLT

Story: Get Wisdom

A Chinese proverb addressing the topic of learning says, "Tell me; I'll forget. Show me; I may remember. But involve me and I'll understand." So much of learning comes from experience. The author of this portion of Proverbs is attempting to impart knowledge and wisdom to his children by writing down important things for them to know in life. I wonder if he ever took the time to actually teach his children by allowing them to see and experience some of the things he wrote about? In Chapter 20, verse 29 the author writes; "The glory of the young is their strength; the gray hair of experience is the splendor of the old. That's a great way of saying that old age brings with it the lessons of experience. When we are young, we should make every attempt to learn from those who have more experience than us. Why should we make all the same mistakes they did? Most adults are more than willing to share their experiences with us so we can live better lives than they did and accomplish greater things. A wise man learns from the mistakes of others.

The following story is a great illustration of learning by experience: A proud young man came to Socrates asking for knowledge. He walked up to the muscular philosopher and said, "O great Socrates, I come to you for knowledge." Socrates recognized a pompous numskull when he saw one. He led the young man through the streets, to the sea, and chest deep into water. Then he asked, "What do you want?"

"Knowledge, O wise Socrates," said the young man with a smile.

Socrates put his strong hands on the man's shoulders and pushed him under. Thirty seconds later Socrates let him up. "What do you want?" he asked again.

"Wisdom," the young man sputtered, "O great and wise Socrates."

Socrates pushed him under again. Thirty seconds passed, thirty-five, forty. Socrates let him up. The man was gasping. "What do you want, young man?"

Between heavy, gasping breaths the fellow wheezed, "Knowledge, O wise and wonderful..."

Socrates jammed him under again. Forty seconds passed, fifty. "What do you want?"

"Air!" the young man screeched. "I need air!"

"When you want knowledge as you have just wanted air, then you will have knowledge."

Proverbs 2:1-5; [1]My child, listen to what I say, and treasure my commands. [2]Tune your ears to wisdom, and concentrate on understanding. [3]Cry out for insight, and ask for understanding. [4]Search for them as you would for silver; seek them like hidden treasures. [5]Then you will understand what it means to fear the Lord, and you will gain knowledge of God.

Application

Purpose of Proverbs

1. Talk about things in life you have to experience firsthand to be able to learn.
   - Example: riding a bike, swimming, receiving the Holy Ghost
2. Discuss some important life lessons you can learn without having to experience.
   - Example: Negative effect of drugs and alcohol, problems of uncontrolled anger.
3. Have a time of family prayer and devotion:
   - Start with praise and worship unto God.
   - Repentance
4. Pray God helps you learn from His Word and from the teaching of others that have wisdom and are willing to share it with you.
   - Remember if we learn from others, we don't have to make all the same mistakes.
5. Commit to read one chapter out of Proverbs each day for the next seven days. There is no better source of wisdom than God's Word! Even better if you read one chapter of Proverbs every single day! It's packed full of wisdom and knowledge.

Family Activity

Box of Wisdom

- Find a box with a lid (a shoe box works great)
- Cut out a square in the top of the box large enough to get your hand inside.
- Cut several pieces of paper into 3 inch squares and pass out several pieces to each family member.
- On the piece of paper write your own proverb. A proverb is a wise saying that is good information for someone to know so they can live life successfully. Everyone, even young children, have learned something valuable in life. Make sure everyone writes 2-3 proverbs.
- Fold up your proverb and place it in the box.
- Take turns pulling out the pieces of paper and reading them off.
- Discuss the words of wisdom and how they can change your life for the better.

Saved from the Fire

Scripture

Take turns reading the following scriptures out loud.

Psalm 18:48-49; [48]He delivers me from my enemies. You also lift me up above those who rise against me; You have delivered me from the violent man. [49]Therefore I will give thanks to You, O Lord, among the Gentiles, And sing praises to Your name. NASB

Daniel 3:16-23; [16]Shadrach, Meshach, and Abednego replied, "O Nebuchadnezzar, we do not need to defend ourselves before you. [17]If we are thrown into the blazing furnace, the God whom we serve is able to save us. He will rescue us from your power, Your Majesty. [18]But even if he doesn't, we want to make it clear to you, Your Majesty, that we will never serve your gods or worship the gold statue you have set up." [19]Nebuchadnezzar was so furious with Shadrach, Meshach, and Abednego that his face became distorted with rage. He commanded that the furnace be heated seven times hotter than usual. [20]Then he ordered some of the strongest men of his army to bind Shadrach, Meshach, and Abednego and throw them into the blazing furnace. [21]So they tied them up and threw them into the furnace, fully dressed in their pants, turbans, robes, and other garments. [22]And because the king, in his anger, had demanded such a hot fire in the furnace, the flames killed the soldiers as they threw the three men in. [23]So Shadrach, Meshach, and Abednego, securely tied, fell into the roaring flames. NLT

Story: The Fiery Furnace

Why didn't God save the three Hebrew boys from going into the fiery furnace in the first place? They trusted in God. They were doing the right thing by refusing to bow down to the king's idol. God should have kept them from going into the furnace, shouldn't He? Just like the three Hebrew boys, we will find out that God does not always keep us from going through the fiery trials in this life. Sometimes He allows us to face the trial and go through the fire to prove that even in these fiery trials He is still in control. Did any of the boys feel betrayed because God did not prevent them from being thrown into the fire? Sometimes we can get upset because God does not do what we think He should do in each situation. Like the three Hebrew boys we need to learn to trust God and do what is right even when God allows us to go through the fire. Notice, as the story continues God knew what He was doing all the time. He delivered the three Hebrew boys, changed the heart of King Nebuchadnezzar, and brought glory to His name!

[24]But suddenly, Nebuchadnezzar jumped up in amazement and exclaimed to his advisers, "Didn't we tie up three men and throw them into the furnace?"

"Yes, Your Majesty, we certainly did," they replied. [25]"Look!" Nebuchadnezzar shouted. "I see four men, unbound, walking around in the fire unharmed! And the fourth looks like a god!"

[26]Then Nebuchadnezzar came as close as he could to the door of the flaming furnace and shouted: "Shadrach, Meshach, and Abednego, servants of the Most High God, come out! Come here!" So Shadrach, Meshach, and Abednego stepped out of the fire. [27]Then the high officers, officials, governors, and advisers crowded around them and saw that the fire had not touched them. Not a hair on their heads was singed, and their clothing was not scorched. They didn't even smell of smoke!

[28]Then Nebuchadnezzar said, "Praise to the God of Shadrach, Meshach, and Abednego! He sent his angel to rescue his servants who trusted in him. They defied the king's command and were willing to die rather than serve or worship any god except their own God. [29]Therefore, I make this decree: If any people, whatever their race or nation or language, speak a word against the God of Shadrach, Meshach, and Abednego, they will be torn limb from limb, and their houses will be turned into heaps of rubble. There is no other god who can rescue like this!"

[30]Then the king promoted Shadrach, Meshach, and Abednego to even higher positions in the province of Babylon.

 **Application**

Saved From the Fire

1. Have you ever been through a trial you thought was not fair or you didn't understand why you were going through the particular trial?
   - Do you think God has an obligation to explain to us why we experience difficult or painful situations in life?

2. Have a time of family prayer and devotion:
   - Start with praise and worship unto God.
   - Repentance

3. Talk about trials you are facing as individuals or as a family right now.

4. Pray God would help you trust in Him regardless of the circumstances.

5. Pray your faith would be increased to the level of the three Hebrew boys; "If we are thrown into the blazing furnace, the God whom we serve is able to save us. He will rescue us from your power, Your Majesty. [18] But even if he doesn't, we want to make it clear to you, Your Majesty, that we will never serve your gods or worship the gold statue you have set up."

 **Family Activity**

S'mores

You will need: chocolate, graham crackers, marshmallows, and something to cook the marshmallow with (a wire clothes hanger works in a pinch).

Heat the marshmallow until it is golden brown on all sides. Sandwich the hot marshmallow with a piece of chocolate between two graham crackers. Enjoy!

If you don't have a fireplace, you can use an outdoor grill or the stove.

When you are looking at the fire, remember the three Hebrew boys! God delivered them from their trial, and He will help you through yours too.

Betrayal

Scripture

Take turns reading the following scriptures out loud.

John 13:18-30; [18]"I am not saying these things to all of you; I know the ones I have chosen. But this fulfills the Scripture that says, 'The one who eats my food has turned against me.' [19] I tell you this beforehand, so that when it happens you will believe that I Am the Messiah. [20]I tell you the truth, anyone who welcomes my messenger is welcoming me, and anyone who welcomes me is welcoming the Father who sent me." [21]Now Jesus was deeply troubled, and he exclaimed, "I tell you the truth, one of you will betray me!" [22]The disciples looked at each other, wondering whom he could mean. [23]The disciple Jesus loved was sitting next to Jesus at the table. [24]Simon Peter motioned to him to ask, "Who's he talking about?" [25]So that disciple leaned over to Jesus and asked, "Lord, who is it?" [26]Jesus responded, "It is the one to whom I give the bread I dip in the bowl." And when he had dipped it, he gave it to Judas, son of Simon Iscariot. [27]When Judas had eaten the bread, Satan entered into him. Then Jesus told him, "Hurry and do what you're going to do." [28]None of the others at the table knew what Jesus meant. [29]Since Judas was their treasurer, some thought Jesus was telling him to go and pay for the food or to give some money to the poor. [30]So Judas left at once, going out into the night. NLT

Story: Power in Forgiveness

At age 14 a young man ran away from home so he could join the military forces that fought in the French and Indian War. At the outbreak of the Revolutionary War, he joined the American army as a colonel and in 1775 shared a command with Ethan Allen in the capture of Ticonderoga. Later he led 1000 men into Canada where he fought in the battle of Quebec. His courage in battle won him a promotion to brigadier general. He was trusted by all of the men who led the American forces against the onslaught of the British armies. But something went wrong in his heart and mind. Thoughts of compromise began to eat away at his patriotic zeal. Soon the unthinkable happened. He offered his services to the British, and in 1780 devised a plan to surrender West Point to British control. Today, instead of being remembered as a national hero, Benedict Arnold is synonymous with "traitor."

Jesus knew what it felt like to be betrayed by someone close to him. Judas Iscariot was one of the twelve men hand chosen by the Lord to join the inner circle of believers that followed Him for three years. Judas was even elevated to a greater position of trust than the other eleven by being assigned the task of safeguarding the money for the group. Jesus and the other disciples trusted Judas, they believed in Judas. He received all the same benefits and honors that the other 11 did while following Jesus.

He saw miracles and was used by God to pray for healing for others and to cast out demons. For reasons unknown, Judas eventually betrayed Jesus for 30 pieces of silver. The final act of betrayal came when Judas kissed Jesus on the cheek in the Garden of Gethsemane, a sign of closeness and compassion used as a sign to those following Judas that Jesus was the one they were to arrest.

The emotional pain that comes from being betrayed is deep and long lasting. The pain is so deep because in order for someone to betray you they must have first gained your trust. When we trust someone it generally means we believe in them; we respect them; we think they will protect us and help us in times of need. The person who betrays someone does exactly the opposite. Just when we need them the most they are not there for us. When we need them to protect us they are the one who hurt us the deepest. Most of us will feel betrayed by someone close to us during this life, a close friend, a family member, a spouse, a minister, and maybe even a parent. All of these are people that may someday betray us. Does that mean we should live the rest of our life guarding ourselves against hurt and pain that may be a result of betrayal? Jesus didn't! He still loved, cared for, ministered to, and loved Judas even though He knew Judas would someday betray Him. We should do the same.

Application

Betrayal

1. Have a time of family prayer and devotion.
2. Start with praise and worship unto God.
3. Have you ever been betrayed or hurt by someone close to you?
   - Have you forgiven them for the betrayal?
4. Take a few minutes and ask God to forgive the person who hurt and betrayed you. Let God know you want to forgive the person for the hurt they caused.
5. Have a time of repentance.
   - You must first forgive others if you expect God to forgive you of your sins (Matthew 5:7).
6. Take turns praying for each other.
7. Pray for any personal needs as a family together.

Family Activity

Eye Spy

- Play this game with at least two players. Go outside to make the game extra interesting.
- Look around and silently select an object that can be seen by all the players.
- Say, "I spy with my little eye," and then give some description of the object, such as "something red," "something square", or "something small."
- Tell the other players to take turns trying to guess what the object is.
- Let the player who correctly guesses the selected item pick the next object, or have all players take turns in a set order (this may be best if you are playing with younger children who may not be so good at guessing).
- Offer extra clues if players are completely stumped.

Fishers of Men

 **Scripture**

Take turns reading the following scriptures out loud.

Matthew 4:18-22; [18]As Jesus was walking beside the Sea of Galilee, he saw two brothers, Simon called Peter and his brother Andrew. They were casting a net into the lake, for they were fishermen. [19]"Come, follow me," Jesus said, "and I will make you fishers of men." [20]At once they left their nets and followed him.

[21]Going on from there, he saw two other brothers, James son of Zebedee and his brother John. They were in a boat with their father Zebedee, preparing their nets. Jesus called them, [22]and immediately they left the boat and their father and followed him. NIV

Story: Hooked on Fishing

I have spent the last four to five years teaching my son and daughter how to fish. It has been a long, sometimes exciting and sometimes annoying process. I must admit they were not real excited about going fishing when they were first approached with the idea. They liked fish, but why couldn't we just go to a store and buy fish like we had before, or go to a restaurant and order it off the menu? I assured them they would have a fun time. We loaded up the fishing poles, tackle box, grabbed a dozen worms from the local store, and headed for the closest lake.

My daughter was squeamish about putting worms on a hook. In fact, she refused to even touch them. "I will hold the pole and you put the worm on daddy", she said. On the other hand, I couldn't get my son to stop playing with the worms. Neither one of them had the foggiest idea how to cast bait out into the water. I had to show them how numerous times and work very closely with them before they were able to successfully get the bait out into the water. After several, "How long is this going to take?" and "I'm bored" statements from them both, we got our first nibble. Tug, tug went the line on the pole. When the fish bit the bait one more time, I hoisted the tip of the pole into the air and set the hook! I passed the pole to one of the kids and let them feel the surge of power the fish exerted on the line and pole as it struggled to get free. Their little hearts raced with excitement. "Slow down, reel it in slowly and easily, take your time." I coached them as they reeled in the fish. Excitement shone in their eyes and their tone of voice shot sky high when they actually saw the first fish, "There it is, there it is! Hurry! Grab the net so it doesn't get away!"

After each of them caught a fish, they were hooked on fishing. Now both of them love to fish and are willing to go every time they are given the opportunity. In fact more often than not, they are begging me to take them fishing. My daughter still doesn't like to touch the worms, but she has no problem taking the fish off the hook. My son still likes to play with the worms, but he hates to touch the fish once they have been caught. They work together as a team. He baits the hook, she unhooks the fish. After several years of fishing, they have caught a variety of different fish: blue gill, trout, catfish, bass, and even sting rays. Fish that ranged in size from tiny little bait fish to whoppers they struggled to reel in. Even though there have been times we went fishing and didn't even get a nibble, their excitement and hopes remain high about going fishing the next time. They are hooked on fishing!

The same trepidation and excitement is also felt in the hearts and minds of individuals that become fishers of men. When Jesus called those first few disciples He told them, "Come, follow me, and I will make you fishers of men." It was the first step to a several year long process of teaching people how to fish for lost souls with the bait of the soul saving gospel. Were there frustrating moments along the way? Were there times when the line got tangled up or the disciples missed the opportunity to set the hook? Yes, there were, but Jesus was a faithful, patient teacher. He realized there would come a day when they would have to fish without Him being there in person to guide their every step. God's desire is for you to become fishers of men. Maybe you have never taken the time to fish in your community for lost souls, maybe you are afraid to touch the bait, but would have no problem caring for the soul once it has been reeled in. Whatever your strength is, God wants you involved in reeling lost souls into the kingdom of God.

 **Application**

Fishers of Men

1. Have a time of family prayer and devotion:
   - Start with praise and worship unto God.
   - Have a time of repentance.
2. Take turns praying for each other.
   - Each person should think of one person that they can invite to church this coming weekend.
3. Ask God to help you be more aware of fishing opportunities (outreach) in your daily life.
   - Make it a point to carry invitation cards with you wherever you go. Pick some up from the church next time you are there.
4. Pray for any personal needs as a family together.

 Family Activity

Go Fish

Setup:
- Seven cards are dealt to each player.
- All remaining cards are placed face down in a draw pile.

To Play:
- The youngest player goes first.
- On your turn, ask a player for a specific card. You must already hold at least one card of the requested rank.
- If the player you ask has any card of the requested rank, he must give all of his cards of that rank to you.
- If you get one or more cards from the player you ask, you get another turn.
- If the person you ask has no relevant cards, they say, "Go fish." You then draw the top card from the draw pile.
- When you collect two cards of the same rank, place the two cards face up in front of yourself.
- The winner is the one who has the most sets of two when the draw pile is gone or when one person no longer holds any more cards.

Parable of the Sower

 **Scripture**
Take turns reading the following scriptures out loud.

Luke 8:4-15; [4]One day Jesus told a story in the form of a parable to a large crowd that had gathered from many towns to hear him: [5]"A farmer went out to plant his seed. As he scattered it across his field, some seed fell on a footpath, where it was stepped on, and the birds ate it. [6]Other seed fell among rocks. It began to grow, but the plant soon wilted and died for lack of moisture. [7]Other seed fell among thorns that grew up with it and choked out the tender plants. [8]Still other seed fell on fertile soil. This seed grew and produced a crop that was a hundred times as much as had been planted!" When he had said this, he called out, "Anyone with ears to hear should listen and understand."

[9]His disciples asked him what this parable meant. [10]He replied, "You are permitted to understand the secrets of the Kingdom of God. But I use parables to teach the others so that the Scriptures might be fulfilled: 'When they look, they won't really see. When they hear, they won't understand.'

[11]"This is the meaning of the parable: The seed is God's word. [12]The seeds that fell on the footpath represent those who hear the message, only to have the devil come and take it away from their hearts and prevent them from believing and being saved. [13]The seeds on the rocky soil represent those who hear the message and receive it with joy. But since they don't have deep roots, they believe for a while, then they fall away when they face temptation. [14]The seeds that fell among the thorns represent those who hear the message, but all too quickly the message is crowded out by the cares and riches and pleasures of this life. And so they never grow into maturity. [15]And the seeds that fell on the good soil represent honest, good-hearted people who hear God's word, cling to it, and patiently produce a huge harvest. NLT

Story: Weed Control

Early one morning a father had gone outside to do some much needed weeding in the small garden that had been planted in the back yard. After several minutes, his eight year old son came out looking for him. "Hey Dad, what are you doing?" the boy asked. Seeing the opportunity to share a story from the Bible with his young son, the father began to talk about the parable of the sower that Jesus told in Luke chapter eight. As dad began to tell the story, the boy knelt down alongside his dad and helped pull some weeds. "The cares of this life are a lot like the weeds we are pulling. The weeds steal necessary water and nutrients that are meant for the plants, just like the cares of this life steal the power and blessing God wants to give us from His Word. If we don't get rid of the weeds, they will take over and we will not get the desired harvest from our garden. In the same manner, if we allow the cares of life to run wild and grow in our lives, we will never see the harvest of spiritual blessing and power that God desires in our life." "Wow Dad!!" said the son, "We should have started pulling these weeds when they were much smaller and fewer in number."

What a powerful statement! The same can be said about the cares of this life. Why is it that the cares of this life have a natural tendency to grow wild and take over complete areas of our lives? How is it we never have the time to give to what is eternally important, but have the time to engage in earthly trivia? The cares of this life have tremendous power to crowd out the precious Word of God and our relationship with Him, only because we allow them to. The best way to deal with the weeds in the garden is to get rid of them when they are small and few in number. The same is true for the cares of life that choke out the Word of God. Get rid of them when they are relatively small and few in number. Keep a constant vigil over your spiritual garden to make sure the things that are growing are things God has planted.

 **Application**

Parable of the Sower

1. Have a time of family prayer and devotion:

2. Sing a worship chorus together that focuses on praising God.
   - "How Great is our God"
   - "Jesus I love you"

3. Have a time of repentance where you focus on asking God to reveal to you the weeds that are growing in your spiritual garden.
   - Ask Him to help you remove them.

4. Ask God to help you focus this week on true priorities of life and not superficial cares of life.

5. Pray for any needs as a family together.

 Family Activity

Seek and Destroy

Walk around your yard and try to find the weeds that are growing.
When you find one give it a name like:
- Golf
- Video Games
- Shopping (pick your store of choice)
- Facebook, Twitter, Instagram
- Surfing the internet
- Gossip
- Ungodly music
- Movies
- Television

(Sorry if I stepped on your toes. I'm not aiming at anyone in particular, but if it stung, maybe you need to pull up the weed and refocus your attention on what God has planted in your life and what He wants you to uproot.)

Ten Commandments

 Scripture
Take turns reading the following scriptures out loud.

Exodus 20:1-17; [1]Then God gave the people all these instructions: [2]I am the Lord your God, who rescued you from the land of Egypt, the place of your slavery. [3]You must not have any other god but me. [4]You must not make for yourself an idol of any kind or an image of anything in the heavens or on the earth or in the sea. [5]You must not bow down to them or worship them, for I, the Lord your God, am a jealous God who will not tolerate your affection for any other gods. I lay the sins of the parents upon their children; the entire family is affected—even children in the third and fourth generations of those who reject me. [6]But I lavish unfailing love for a thousand generations on those who love me and obey my commands. [7]You must not misuse the name of the Lord your God. The Lord will not let you go unpunished if you misuse his name. [8]Remember to observe the Sabbath day by keeping it holy. [9]You have six days each week for your ordinary work, [10]but the seventh day is a Sabbath day of rest dedicated to the Lord your God. On that day no one in your household may do any work. This includes you, your sons and daughters, your male and female servants, your livestock, and any foreigners living among you. [11]For in six days the Lord made the heavens, the earth, the sea, and everything in them; but on the seventh day he rested. That is why the Lord blessed the Sabbath day and set it apart as holy. [12]Honor your father and mother. Then you will live a long, full life in the land the Lord your God is giving you. [13]You must not murder. [14]You must not commit adultery. [15]You must not steal. [16]You must not testify falsely against your neighbor. [17]You must not covet your neighbor's house. You must not covet your neighbor's wife, male or female servant, ox or donkey, or anything else that belongs to your neighbor. NLT

Story: Write Them on Your Heart

Everything about the Ten Commandments suggests it was a text intended to be memorized and publicly recited by God's people. Notice, the Ten Commandments are equal in number to the fingers of both hands therefore helping someone to be able to recall all of them.

David said in Psalm 119:11-16; [11]I have hidden your word in my heart, that I might not sin against you. [12]I praise you, O Lord; teach me your decrees. [13]I have recited aloud all the regulations you have given us. [14]I have rejoiced in your laws as much as in riches. [15]I will study your commandments and reflect on your ways. [16]I will delight in your decrees and not forget your word.

The importance of memorizing foundational components of the Word of God is essential to our Christian walk. If our goal is to please Him

in everything we do, we have to know what pleases Him. We cannot carry a Bible with us everywhere we go and stop and look up how we should respond in each and every situation. We have to memorize God's Word so we will know instantly how to respond in a manner that brings glory and honor to God. If the people of God do not know the foundational message of the Bible, how are we expected to show a world in darkness this beautiful light we have inside of us; the ever present power of God's Spirit manifest in us.

A Sunday school teacher was discussing the Ten Commandments with five and six year olds. After explaining the commandment to "Honor thy Father and thy Mother," she asked, "Is there a commandment that teaches us how to treat our brothers and sisters?"

Without missing a beat, one little boy (the oldest of a family) answered, "Thou shall not kill."

 **Application**

Ten Commandments

1. Have a time of family prayer and devotion:
   - Start with praise and worship.
   - Have a time of repentance.
2. With someone leading, repeat the Ten Commandments out loud as a family.
3. Spend some time praying the Ten Commandments. Use them as an outline to help direct your family prayer.
4. Pray for any needs as a family together.

 **Family Activity**

Ten Commandments Craft

Make your own copy of the Ten Commandments to post somewhere in the house so everyone can see them and work at memorizing them.

Use construction paper and draw two tablets of stone. Either write them by hand or use a special font from the computer and put five commandments on each stone. Try to make them look really nice. Make sure everyone has a part in the activity.

Children's Ten Commandments:
1. Thou shalt have no other gods before me.
2. Thou shalt not make unto thee any graven image.
3. Thou shalt not take the name of the Lord thy God in vain.
4. Remember the Sabbath day, to keep it holy.
5. Honor thy father and thy mother.
6. Thou shalt not kill.
7. Thou shalt not commit adultery.
8. Thou shalt not steal.
9. Thou shalt not bear false witness against thy neighbor.
10. Thou shalt not covet.

Guard Your Eyes

 ## Scripture

Take turns reading the following scriptures out loud.

1 John 2:16; For the world offers only a craving for physical pleasure, a craving for everything we see, and pride in our achievements and possessions. These are not from the Father, but are from this world. NLT

Psalm 101: 2-4; [2]I will be careful to live a blameless life—when will you come to help me? I will lead a life of integrity in my own home. [3]I will refuse to look at anything vile and vulgar. I hate all who deal crookedly; I will have nothing to do with them. [4]I will reject perverse ideas and stay away from every evil. NKJV

1 John 2:15-17; [15]Love not the world, neither the things that are in the world. If any man love the world, the love of the Father is not in him. [16]For all that is in the world, the lust of the flesh, and the lust of the eyes, and the pride of life, is not of the Father, but is of the world. [17]And the world passeth away, and the lust thereof: but he that doeth the will of God abideth for ever. KJV

Story: Be Wise... Protect Your Eyes

Statistics report:
- Children spend more time watching television than in any other activity except sleep.
- 54% of kids have a TV in their bedroom
- 44% of kids say they watch something different when they're alone than with their parents (25% choose MTV)
- 66% of children (ages 10 to 16) surveyed say that their peers are influenced by TV shows
- 62% say that sex on TV shows and movies influences kids to have sex when they are too young
- 77% say there is too much sex before marriage on television
- 65% say that shows like The Simpsons and Married With Children encourage kids to disrespect parents
- Witnessing repeated violent acts can lead to desensitization and a lack of empathy for human suffering
- Television alone is responsible for 10% of youth violence. Leonard Eron, Senior Research Scientist at the University of Michigan

All of the statistical information above was taken from a research study titled "Television and Socialization of Young Children" completed by the University of Kansas.

Science has confirmed the power of the eye upon the mind. It is reported that 90% of our thought life is stimulated by what we view through our eyes. 65% of what we see is registered in our long term memory, while only 15% of what we hear ever makes it to long term memory.

By age 18, a U.S. youth will have seen 16,000 simulated murders and 200,000 acts of violence. - American Psychiatric Association

Research has shown that "mindless" television or video games may idle and impoverish the development of the pre-frontal cortex, or that portion of the brain responsible for planning, organizing, and sequencing behavior for self-control, moral judgment, and attention. - American Academy of Pediatrics - Understanding TV's Effects on the Developing Brain, Jane M. Healy, Ph.D.

If you missed the point of this family devotion please re-read the scriptures this devotion started with!

 **Application**

Guard Your Eyes

1. Have a time of family prayer and devotion.
2. Start with praise and worship unto God.
3. Pray and ask God to help reveal things in your life that have a negative influence on your spirit.
4. Talk about the things you have seen that have influenced your thoughts or behavior in a negative way.
   - Is there anything you need to get rid of to ensure "No evil thing has been set before your eye?"
5. Pray God would help lead and direct you in cleansing your home of negative visual influences.
6. Pray for any personal needs as a family together.

 **Family Activity**

Family Game Night

Monopoly, Uno, Life, Yahtzee, Sorry, etc.

Many parents turn to entertainment or video games to be the caretakers of their children. Let's admit it! At times it is just plain easier to have kid's park themselves in front of something that has their attention, be it videos, computer, or video games. These things cannot and will not replace the personal attention that kids need from their parents. Take an hour to spend personal time with your family and play a good old fashioned board game.

Make it exciting, fun, and create memories.

Hair

Scripture

Take turns reading the following scriptures out loud.

1 Corinthians 11:2-16; [2]I am so glad that you always keep me in your thoughts, and that you are following the teachings I passed on to you. [3]But there is one thing I want you to know: The head of every man is Christ, the head of woman is man, and the head of Christ is God. [4]A man dishonors his head if he covers his head while praying or prophesying. [5]But a woman dishonors her head if she prays or prophesies without a covering on her head, for this is the same as shaving her head. [6]Yes, if she refuses to wear a head covering, she should cut off all her hair! But since it is shameful for a woman to have her hair cut or her head shaved, she should wear a covering. [7]A man should not wear anything on his head when worshiping, for man is made in God's image and reflects God's glory. And woman reflects man's glory. [8]For the first man didn't come from woman, but the first woman came from man. [9]And man was not made for woman, but woman was made for man. [10]For this reason, and because the angels are watching, a woman should wear a covering on her head to show she is under authority. [11]But among the Lord's people, women are not independent of men, and men are not independent of women. [12]For although the first woman came from man, every other man was born from a woman, and everything comes from God. [13]Judge for yourselves. Is it right for a woman to pray to God in public without covering her head? [14]Isn't it obvious that it's disgraceful for a man to have long hair? [15]And isn't long hair a woman's pride and joy? For it has been given to her as a covering. [16]But if anyone wants to argue about this, I simply say that we have no other custom than this, and neither do God's other churches. NLT

Story: **Your Glory**

What is communicated by a stop sign? Obviously the command to stop is given, but why? The sign itself offers no explanation as to the reason "why" behind it. The reason for the stop sign is supposed to be understood if a person is able to drive. The reason for posting a stop sign is so the driver will stop, look both ways, and then respond to the traffic that may or may not be present on the road, in a safe manner. There are hundreds of traffic laws in place for the purpose of assisting individuals to get from point A to point B safely. If everyone just did what they wanted and showed no respect for traffic laws there would be a tremendous amount of accidents. Let's face it; many people only stop at the stop sign because they are afraid of getting a ticket from a police officer. It is fear of local authority that motivates some people to obedience. For those who are law abiding citizens who believe in the rules of the road, they stop because the sign represents order and justice in their world.

Scripture states that a woman is to have long hair and that a man is to have his hair kept short. The importance of the teaching is in the reasoning behind it. The individual who is obedient to this command is showing their submission to God and his plan for leadership. An individual with a submissive and reverent heart will obey the custom because they respect the one who has given the command, God.

People will argue that Paul was only providing this information because it fit with the customs of the day in the city of Corinth. Therefore, there is no reason for the modern day church in America to conform to the teachings that he provides in this portion of scripture. I guess those that argue that point would be right if their ultimate judge and most important influence in their life was society. But, I must remind you that we are strangers in a foreign land, pilgrims on a journey whose ultimate destination is the eternal glory of God's abode in the heavens. Therefore, we should obey Paul's teaching to the church and submit ourselves to God's plan of authority. There is a bigger picture!

 **Application**

Hair

1. Have a time of family prayer and devotion:
   - Start with praise and worship unto God.
   - Ask God to forgive you of any sin in your life.

2. Name the people in your life that are authority figures that you should respect and submit yourself to.

3. Pray and ask God to give these people wisdom to lead and direct you and God's church.

4. Pray and ask God to help you submit to the individuals you listed above.

5. Pray God would give you wisdom and humility to submit to His plans and desires for your life.

6. Pray for any personal needs as a family together.

 Family Activity

Crazy Hair Night

- Have a contest to see who can create the craziest hair style.
- Next allow someone to give you a crazy hair style.
- See who comes up with the most creative and crazy hair style.

Holding Your Tongue

Scripture

Take turns reading the following scriptures out loud.

James 3:2-12; [2]Indeed, we all make many mistakes. For if we could control our tongues, we would be perfect and could also control ourselves in every other way. [3]We can make a large horse go wherever we want by means of a small bit in its mouth. [4]And a small rudder makes a huge ship turn wherever the pilot chooses to go, even though the winds are strong. [5]In the same way, the tongue is a small thing that makes grand speeches. But a tiny spark can set a great forest on fire. [6]And the tongue is a flame of fire. It is a whole world of wickedness, corrupting your entire body. It can set your whole life on fire, for it is set on fire by hell itself. [7]People can tame all kinds of animals, birds, reptiles, and fish, [8]but no one can tame the tongue. It is restless and evil, full of deadly poison. [9]Sometimes it praises our Lord and Father, and sometimes it curses those who have been made in the image of God. [10]And so blessing and cursing come pouring out of the same mouth. Surely, my brothers and sisters, this is not right! [11]Does a spring of water bubble out with both fresh water and bitter water? [12]Does a fig tree produce olives, or a grapevine produce figs? No, and you can't draw fresh water from a salty spring. NLT

Story: Words Can Hurt or Heal

A sharp tongue is the only edged tool that grows sharper with constant use.

A man working in the produce department was asked by a lady if she could buy half a head of lettuce. He replied, "Half a head? Are you serious? God grows these in whole heads and that's how we sell them!"

"You mean," she persisted, "that after all the years I've shopped here, you won't sell me half-a-head of lettuce?"

"Look," he said, "If you like, I'll ask the manager."

She indicated that would be appreciated, so the young man marched to the front of the store. "You won't believe this, but there's a lame-brained idiot of a lady back there who wants to know if she can buy half-a-head of lettuce."

He noticed the manager gesturing, and turned around to see the lady standing behind him, obviously having followed him to the front of the store. "And this nice lady was wondering if she could buy the other half," he concluded.

Later in the day the manager cornered the young man and said, "That was the finest example of thinking on your feet I've ever seen! Where did you learn that?" "I grew up in Grand Rapids, and if you know anything about Grand Rapids, you know that it's known for its great hockey teams and its ugly women."

The manager's face flushed, and he interrupted, "My wife is from Grand Rapids!" "And which hockey team did she play for?"

James says amazing things about the power of the tongue and the inability of man to control it. By nature it is a world of wickedness, corrupt, full of deadly poison, and set on fire by hell itself. Jesus said in Matthew 15:18 that the things that come out of your mouth are actually verbally revealing of what is held within your heart. We must be careful to think before we speak. The little saying, "Sticks and stones may break my bones, but words will never hurt me" does not hold any truth. Words do hurt. The spoken word can harm not only the hearer, but also the speaker. We may say some of the dumbest things that we will regret uttering for the rest of our life. Paul tells us, "Let your conversation be gracious and attractive so that you will have the right response for everyone."

King David realized the power of the tongue and his own personal inability to control it when he wrote in Psalm 143, "Set a guard, O Lord, over my mouth; Keep watch over the door of my lips. Do not incline my heart to any evil thing."

One of my personal favorites is what James writes, "Sometimes it praises our Lord and Father, and sometimes it curses those who have been made in the image of God. And so blessing and cursing come pouring out of the same mouth. Surely, my brothers and sisters, this is not right!"

Holding Your Tongue

1. Have a time of family prayer and devotion:
   - Start with praise and worship unto God.
   - Pray and ask God to forgive you of your wrong words and actions. Ask Him to wash away any sin that may be in your heart.
2. Pray and ask God to help you have better control of your tongue.
3. Talk about the things you have said that might have been hurtful to others.
   - Did you really feel in your heart what was spoken by your mouth?
   - Do you need to ask someone to forgive you for the negative words you have spoken to them or about them?
4. Pray that God would help you to speak positive, uplifting words to those around you.
5. Pray for any personal needs as a family together.

 Family Activity

I Am

(Marco Polo with a Positive Spin)

- Find a fairly large area outside or several rooms inside that do not contain many breakable items. Use this area as the playing field.
- Tie a scarf around the eyes of the person who will be IT first. Make sure they are unable to see. Spin them around 3 to 5 times and let them go.
- When the person who is IT says "I AM" everyone else must say something good about the person. The person who is IT must find the other players and tag one of them. The person who is tagged must now be IT. The best way to teach ourselves to think and say positive things is to actually do it. Have fun!

Repentance

Scripture

Take turns reading the following scriptures out loud.

Luke 10:8-16; ⁸If you enter a town and it welcomes you, eat whatever is set before you. ⁹Heal the sick, and tell them, 'The Kingdom of God is near you now.' ¹⁰But if a town refuses to welcome you, go out into its streets and say, ¹¹'We wipe even the dust of your town from our feet to show that we have abandoned you to your fate. And know this—the Kingdom of God is near!' ¹²I assure you, even wicked Sodom will be better off than such a town on judgment day. ¹³What sorrow awaits you, Korazin and Bethsaida! For if the miracles I did in you had been done in wicked Tyre and Sidon, their people would have repented of their sins long ago, clothing themselves in burlap and throwing ashes on their heads to show their remorse. ¹⁴Yes, Tyre and Sidon will be better off on judgment day than you. ¹⁵And you people of Capernaum, will you be honored in heaven? No, you will go down to the place of the dead. ¹⁶Then he said to the disciples, "Anyone who accepts your message is also accepting me. And anyone who rejects you is rejecting me. And anyone who rejects me is rejecting God, who sent me." NLT

Psalm 51:17; The sacrifice you desire is a broken spirit. You will not reject a broken and repentant heart, O God. NLT

Story: Repentance = Change

Wabush, a town in a remote portion of Canada, was completely isolated for some time. After many years of isolation, a road was cut through the wilderness to reach it. Wabush now has one road leading into it, and thus, only one road leading out. If someone would travel the unpaved road for six to eight hours to get into Wabush, there is only one way he or she could leave - by turning around.

Each of us, at birth, arrives in a town called Sin. As in Wabush, there is only one way out - a road built by God himself. But in order to take that road, one must first turn around. That complete about face is what the Bible calls repentance, and without it, there's no way out of the town of Sin.

While an elder missionary was serving in South Africa, a young Dutchman came into the Sunday morning service. During the preaching, God spoke to his heart and convicted him of sin. The next morning he went to the beautiful home of another Dutchman and said to him, "Do you recognize this old watch?"

"Why, yes," answered the other. "Those are my initials; that is my watch. I lost it eight years ago. How did you get it, and how long have you had it?"

"I stole it," was the reply.

"What made you bring it back now?"

"I was converted last night," was the answer, "and I have brought it back first thing this morning. If you would have been awake, I would have brought it last night."

Repentance is more than a feeling or a belief. Repentance is a mixture of feelings and actions. To say you are sorry and not change your behavior really means you were never sorry in the first place. True repentance always produces the fruit of changed behavior. My mother would always ask me, "Are you truly sorry for what you did or are you just sorry you got caught?"

Jesus has given you and I the most amazing opportunity to repent of our sins and seek His grace and mercy. Jesus says the people who hear His Word, understand what He has to offer, and still choose to reject His mercy will suffer greatly. Even the people of Sodom who chose wickedness over morality will be better off on the Day of Judgment than those who reject His message of grace and forgiveness. Wow! Sounds like you have a choice between being sorry now and repenting or being sorry you got caught without mercy and grace on the Day of Judgment. Choose to have a repentant heart; it's easier in the long run, and it will make all the difference on judgment day.

 **Application**

Repentance

1. Have a time of family prayer and devotion:
   - Start with praise and worship unto God.
   - Pray and ask God to forgive you of any sin you may have committed.
2. Ask God to give you the wisdom to overcome sin in your life that has become repetitive (sin that you have to continually ask forgiveness for.)
3. Pray God would direct you to someone you can confess your weakness to.
   - James 5:16; Therefore confess your sins to each other and pray for each other so that you may be healed. The prayer of a righteous man is powerful and effective.
4. Pray for any personal needs as a family together.

 **Family Activity**

Paper Balls

Crumple about 10-15 sheets of paper into balls. Divide everyone into two teams and have them stand at opposite sides of the room. Mark the center of the floor with masking tape (or a blanket folded up length wise) to separate each team.

The paper balls represents sin, the goal of the game is to throw the sin on the other teams side of the room. After one minute the team with the least sin (paper balls) is the winner. Switch the teams around and play again.

When we have Jesus in our lives He gives us the strength and help we need to get rid of all our sins. However, being a Christian does not mean we are completely free of sin. Temptation is the vehicle that brings sin into our lives. Sometimes there are temptations, such as envy, anger, disobedience, and other garbage of which we need to be aware of. The goal of temptation is to get our focus off of Jesus and on this world. When we are faced with temptation, we need to treat it like the paper ball and throw it away as fast as possible.

Dedication

Scripture
Take turns reading the following scriptures out loud.

Acts 13:2-3; [2]One day as these men were worshiping the Lord and fasting, the Holy Spirit said, "Dedicate Barnabas and Saul for the special work to which I have called them." [3]So after more fasting and prayer, the men laid their hands on them and sent them on their way. NLT

Philippians 1:6; For I am confident of this very thing, that He who began a good work in you will perfect it until the day of Christ Jesus. NASB

Story: Mission Accomplished

It does not take great men to do great things; it only takes consecrated men.

Lieutenant Colonel Terence Otway, commander of the 9th Parachute Battalion of the British 6th Airborne Division, had an assignment to destroy the four powerful guns of a coastal battery in Merville, overlooking Sword Beach. If the 9th could not complete the task on time, naval gunfire would try. The bombardment was to begin at 5:30 a.m.

Otway had an elaborate strategy to overrun the guns, but the plan misfired. An initial air attack was a total failure, and then his battalion was dropped across almost 50 miles off the countryside. Of his 700-man battalion, Otway could find only 150 soldiers. Nevertheless, the men improvised brilliantly. They cut gaps through the outer barricade of the gun battery with wire cutters. One group cleared a path through the minefields, crawling on hands and knees while feeling for tripwires and prodding the ground ahead with bayonets. Now they waited for the order to attack. Otway knew casualties would be high, but the guns had to be silenced. "Everybody in!", he yelled. "We're going to take this bloody battery!" And in they went.

Red flares burst over their heads, and machine-gun fire poured out to meet them. Through the deadly barrage, the paratroopers crawled, ran, dropped, and ran some more. Mines exploded. There were yells and screams and the flash of grenades as paratroopers piled into trenches and fought hand to hand with the enemy.

Germans began surrendering. Lt. Michael Dowling and his men knocked out the four guns. Then Dowling found Otway. He stood before his colonel, his right hand holding the left side of his chest. "Battery taken as ordered, sir," Dowling declared. The battle had lasted just 15 minutes. Otway fired a yellow flare - the success signal - just fifteen minutes before the naval bombardment was to start. Moments later Otway found Dowling's lifeless body. He had been dying at the time he made his report.

Dedication is defined as complete and whole hearted devotion, the willingness to commit yourself to the completion of a task even if there is the possibility of losing your life in the process. The great Apostle Paul knows firsthand what dedication requires of an individual. He had dedicated his life to fulfilling God's purpose and plan. Little did Paul know that in the process of doing God's work he would be put through some pretty terrible situations:

- 5 times he was whipped
- 3 times he was beaten with a rod
- Once he was stoned
- He was shipwrecked three times
- Lost at sea once
- Threatened to be killed by literally every one you could possibly think of
- Left hungry, cold, and at times naked
- Burdened with the daily stress of being the pastor of numerous churches.

Despite all the unfortunate circumstances Paul had to go through in his life, moments before he passed from this life I can imagine Paul lifting his eyes to heaven and saying, "Lord, mission accomplished! The work you began in me is now complete."

It does not take great men or women to do great things; it only takes consecrated men and women.

Dedication

1. Have a time of family prayer and devotion:
   - Start with praise and worship unto God.
   - Ask God to forgive you of any sin in your life.

2. Pray God would give you personal strength to live your life completely dedicated and consecrated to Him.

3. What one thing can you do this week to improve on your personal dedication to God?
   - Be more consistent in reading God's Word.
   - Daily prayer
   - Being mindful of those around you that you might be able to witness to about the love and mercy of God.

4. Pray for any personal needs as a family together.

 **Family Activity**

Family Walk and Talk

As a family, go for a walk around your neighborhood. As you walk talk about different people you personally know or have heard about that have dedicated their lives to a specific cause:
- Missionaries
- Evangelist
- Pastors
- Fire fighters
- Military personnel
- Educators

Discuss what "cause" these people have dedicated their lives to, and how your family can become more dedicated to the cause of Christ in your life and in your neighborhood.

Do You Know The Word?

 Scripture
Take turns reading the following scriptures out loud.

Psalm 119:9-16; ⁹How can a young man keep his way pure? By keeping it according to Your word. ¹⁰With all my heart I have sought You; Do not let me wander from Your commandments. ¹¹Your word I have treasured in my heart, That I may not sin against You. ¹²Blessed are You, O Lord; Teach me Your statutes. ¹³With my lips I have told of All the ordinances of Your mouth. ¹⁴I have rejoiced in the way of Your testimonies, As much as in all riches. ¹⁵I will meditate on Your precepts and regard Your ways. ¹⁶I shall delight in Your statutes; I shall not forget Your word. NASB

Story: Road Map to Heaven

Has America lost so much of what originally made this country stand apart from all others and helped propel it towards greatness? As a country, our belief in God and our founding fathers reverence for God's Word played a significant role in laying the foundation for this great country. Where are we now? Have we fallen away from those principle beliefs in God and His Word as a country? Former Secretary of Education William Bennett concludes that, "We have become the kind of society civilized countries used to send missionaries to." In fact there are numerous Christian organizations from places like India, Africa, and numerous countries of South America that have sent missionaries to America to evangelize and help turn it back toward God.

Pollster George Gallup Jr. has long referred to America as a "nation of biblical illiterates". Only four in ten Americans know Jesus delivered the Sermon on the Mount. A majority of citizens cannot name the four Gospels of the New Testament: Matthew, Mark, Luke and John. Only three in ten teenagers know Easter is a celebration of the resurrection of our Lord Jesus Christ from the grave. Two-thirds of Americans believe there are few, if any, absolute principles to direct human behavior.

How do we get this country back to what made it great? Is it even possible to return to the solid Biblical principles that once propelled us to greatness? I hope the answer is yes. The most important thing you can do is make sure you have a solid understanding of God's Word. Hide God's Word within you like David did in Psalm 199:11 "Thy Word have I hid in mine heart, that I might not sin against thee." Make a daily effort to memorize portions of God's Word, you will find it will work like a road map to direct and guide your life.

Think of God's Word as an absolutely accurate map. A map tells you how to get to a certain destination, but just looking at a map won't automatically transport you to Arizona, England, or Peru. Getting to these places means you have to make effort, pay the cost, take the time for travel, and stay at it until you arrive. The Christian life requires us to persevere and daily follow God's map for our life.

Almost half of Christians today believe in the existence of UFOs. Are UFOs real? To answer that question it is sometimes best to ask another question? Does the Word of God say anything about UFOs, do I need to believe in them to make it to heaven, or to direct the lost to Jesus? The answer to the question is a loud and audible NO! We need to have a clear understanding of God's Word and position His Word as the divine authority in our life. Let God's Word be your guide.

 **Application**

Do You Know The Word?

1. Have a time of family prayer and devotion:
   - Start with praise and worship unto God.

2. Grab a Bible and take turns reading Psalm 119:1-48.
   - Talk about what you think David's main point is in this passage of scripture.
   - What verse or verses stood out most to you?

3. Ask God to forgive you of any sin in your life.

4. Pray that God would put a hunger for His Word into your heart and soul.

5. Pray out loud: Psalm 42:1, As the deer pants for the water brooks, So pants my soul for You, O God.

6. Pray for any personal needs as a family together.

 **Family Activity**

Animal Sound Sword Drill

Each of the following verses contain a reference to an animal. As soon as the children find the verse, they need to act or make sounds like the animal mentioned. The first one to do this gets a point.

Here are some suitable references:
- Philippians 3:2 [Dogs]
- Esther 6:8 [Horse]
- 1 Corinthians 10:9 [Serpent]
- Proverbs 17:12 [Bear]
- Zechariah 13:5 [Cattle]
- Matthew 8:30 [Swine or Pigs]
- Genesis 29:2 [Sheep]
- Psalm 105:30 [Frogs]
- Judges 14:5 [Lions]
- Luke 12:6 [Sparrows]

Reverence for God's Presence

Scripture

Take turns reading the following scriptures out loud.

Proverbs 1:7; The fear of the LORD is the beginning of knowledge: but fools despise wisdom and instruction. KJV

Story: Don't Neglect God

In 1 Samuel 4; Israel was at war with the Philistines. The Israelite army was camped near Ebenezer (Stone of Help), and the Philistines were at Aphek. The Philistines attacked and defeated the army of Israel, killing 4,000 men. After the battle was over, the troops retreated to their camp, and the elders of Israel asked, "Why did the Lord allow us to be defeated by the Philistines?" Then they said, "Let's bring the Ark of the Covenant of the Lord from Shiloh. If we carry it into battle with us, it will save us from our enemies."

The people of Israel treated the Ark and presence of God as a sort of good luck charm, a lucky rabbit's foot or horse-shoe. The reverence and respect for the vessel that holds God's Glory was not what it should have been. If the Ark was to be in battle with them, why was it not there in the first place? It was not until they got desperate and realized they were unable to defeat the enemy that they turned to the Ark; the earthly throne for God's presence.

So, they sent men to Shiloh to bring the Ark of the Covenant. Hophni and Phinehas, the sons of Eli, were also there with the Ark of the Covenant of God. When all Israel saw the Ark of the Covenant of the Lord coming into the camp, their shout of joy was so loud it made the ground shake! "What's going on?" the Philistines asked. "What's all the shouting about in the Hebrew camp?" When they were told the Ark of the Lord had arrived, they panicked. "The gods have come into their camp!" they cried. "This is a disaster! We have never had to face anything like this before! Who can save us from these mighty gods of Israel? They are the same gods who destroyed the Egyptians with plagues when Israel was in the wilderness."

It appeared the Philistines had a greater reverence for the God of Israel and what He was capable of doing than the Israelites did. The heathen Philistines shook in fear of what God was able to accomplish. They knew their only hope was to fight with all their might.

The Philistines fought desperately, and Israel was defeated again. The slaughter was great; 30,000 Israelite soldiers died that day. The Ark of God was captured, and Hophni and Phinehas, the two sons of Eli, were killed. A messenger ran from the battlefield and arrived at Shiloh later that same day. "Israel has been defeated by the Philistines," a messenger told Eli the priest. "The people have been slaughtered, and your two sons, Hophni and Phinehas, were also killed, and the Ark of God has been captured." When Eli heard the Ark of the Lord had been captured, he fell backward from his seat beside the gate. He broke his neck and died. Eli's daughter-in-law, the wife of Phinehas, was pregnant and near her time of delivery. When she heard the Ark of God had been captured and that her father-in-law and husband were dead, she went into labor and gave birth. She died in childbirth, but before she passed away the midwives tried to encourage her. "Don't be afraid," they said. "You have a baby boy!" But she did not answer or pay attention to them. She named the child Ichabod (meaning the glory has departed), for she said, "Israel's glory is gone."

30,000 soldiers, three priests, and one mother died of extreme grief the day the ark was taken. 30,004 people all died in one day because Israel was treating Him like a good luck charm instead of reverencing and respecting His presence or the vessel that was His earthly throne. Israel brought God out to fight their battle for them when things got desperate, but they would not show reverence and worship Him back at the tabernacle. It appears God said, I would rather be in the presence of a heathen people who reverence and respect me than with a group of people that treat me as a good luck charm when things in life get difficult.

What about you? Do you love and serve Him all the time, or do you only call upon God when things are not going right in your life?

 **Application**

Reverence for God's Presence

1. Have a time of family prayer and devotion.
   - Start with praise and worship unto God.

2. Spend an extended amount of time focusing on praise and worship.
   - Play a song that focuses on worship or if you have musical instruments play a song while everyone worships and praises God.

3. Ask God to forgive you of any sin in your life.

4. What can you do to make sure you are not treating God like Israel did in the story from 1 Samuel chapter 4?
   - Talk about how as a family you will continually reverence God's presence.

5. Pray for any personal needs as a family together.

 **Family Activity**

Crazy Praise Night

Find as many musical instruments as possible. Go to a .99 cent store to buy instruments beforehand if possible.

Make sure everyone has something to play. Get creative if necessary. Use pots and pans, toys, or the two hands God provided for you to clap unto the Lord.

Choose a worship chorus everyone in the home knows and do your best to play and sing unto the Lord.

Now do the same song again but sing it in one of the following music styles:
- Country Western
- Blues
- Rap
- Opera
- Create your own style

You Are the Light

Scripture

Take turns reading the following scriptures out loud.

Matthew 5:14-16; [14]You are the light of the world. A city that is set on a hill cannot be hidden. [15]Nor do they light a lamp and put it under a basket, but on a lampstand, and it gives light to all who are in the house. [16]Let your light so shine before men, that they may see your good works and glorify your Father in heaven. NLT

Story: How Bright is Your Light?

The door creaked open and Daniel and Josh walked into the room. The loud music reverberating through the little coffee shop made it difficult to concentrate, even hear what they tried to say to each other. They chose the table at the very back of the room, farthest from the blaring music, so they could hold a decent conversation. Daniel and Josh attended the same school and had several classes together. Josh was one of the more popular students at school. He was involved in a variety of activities, and there was always a group of people clamoring around him for attention. Still, with all the crowds and multitude of activities, Josh felt very lonely inside. He came to realize filling his life with activity and people only supplied a temporary band-aid for his internal loneliness. Josh and Daniel never spoke much to each other before this day, but that was all about to change dramatically.

"Daniel," Josh said, "I've noticed that you always appear to be so comfortable with yourself, you always seem so at ease regardless of who is around or who is not. I've watched you for weeks and you never get very upset or freak out when things don't go right. What's up?"

"You have to be kidding me." said Daniel, "You're the popular, self confident one involved in all the after school activities. Why would you be watching me?"

"Because you're different, you stand out from everyone else," Josh said, "You don't talk dirty or tell dirty jokes like the other guys, and it seems you have a way of making those around you feel better about themselves. I have to be honest with you Daniel. I'm jealous of what you have. I just don't know what it is that makes you so different."

Daniel, "Oh, I know what you are talking about. It's God! I know who God is!"

Daniel stopped to reflect upon what he might have done to attract the attention of Josh. Daniel never stopped to witness to him or any of the people Josh associated with. Daniel didn't wear a shirt, button, or place stickers on his folder that proclaimed his belief in God identifying him as a Christian. Just then, the light hanging from the ceiling caught Daniel's attention. It was the only source of light in the whole coffee shop, yet it provided adequate lighting for everyone to see. The light did not flash off and on, it did not project bright beams of neon colored light, it just shined. That's all it did! But shining was what it was made to do. Daniel realized that just being who God made him to be made him stand out amidst everyone else. Daniel didn't have to do anything flashy. He didn't have to stand on a box in the middle of the school and preach the gospel. He didn't have to wear a t-shirt that let people around him know he was a Christian. He is the living breathing gospel, walking right in the middle of all the kids at school. When he submits his human spirit to the Spirit of God and allows the light of God's Spirit to shine through him, it sends off an illumination of the Holy Ghost that pierces the dark and empty hearts of those around him that do not know Jesus Christ. The song he learned years ago as a little boy in Sunday school, "This little light of mine, I'm gonna let it shine", now became a reality in his life.

"All I have to do is let it shine," He said out loud. "What did you say," asked Josh? "Oh, nothing," Daniel replied. "Josh, to be honest with you, the one thing different between me and most of the other kids at school is my relationship with Jesus."

As the conversation carried on, the room appeared to get brighter and brighter, not from the little light hanging from the middle of the ceiling, but from the light illuminating from Daniel.

 **Application**

You Are the Light

1. Have a time of family prayer and devotion:
   - Start with praise and worship unto God.
   - Ask God to forgive you of any sin in your life.
2. Name places you go to where the light of God's Spirit needs to shine.
3. What are some things you could do to allow God's light to shine in your world?
4. Pray and ask God to help you act in a way wherever you go that allows His light to shine.
5. Pray God would give you wisdom and humility to submit to His plans and desires for your life.
6. Pray for any personal needs as a family together.

 Family Activity

Flashlight Tag

- Turn most of the lights off in the house.
- One person gets a flashlight while the rest of the family runs.
- When the light hits someone they are it.

Notice how difficult it is to get around safely without the light, while the one with the flashlight has no problems at all finding their way around safely.

Compare this to walking in this world without the light of Jesus shining through us. It's His light that will help lead us through difficult and dangerous times.

Drawing a Line

Scripture

Take turns reading the following scriptures out loud.

Exodus 19:9-12; [9]Then the Lord said to Moses, "I will come to you in a thick cloud, Moses, so the people themselves can hear me when I speak with you. Then they will always trust you." Moses told the Lord what the people had said. [10]Then the Lord told Moses, "Go down and prepare the people for my arrival. Consecrate them today and tomorrow, and have them wash their clothing. [11]Be sure they are ready on the third day, for on that day the Lord will come down on Mount Sinai as all the people watch. [12]Mark off a boundary all around the mountain. Warn the people, 'Be careful! Do not go up on the mountain or even touch its boundaries. Anyone who touches the mountain will certainly be put to death. NLT

Ephesians 4:11-15; [11]Now these are the gifts Christ gave to the church: the apostles, the prophets, the evangelists, and the pastors and teachers. [12]Their responsibility is to equip God's people to do his work and build up the church, the body of Christ. [13]This will continue until we all come to such unity in our faith and knowledge of God's Son that we will be mature in the Lord, measuring up to the full and complete standard of Christ. [14]Then we will no longer be immature like children. We won't be tossed and blown about by every wind of new teaching. We will not be influenced when people try to trick us with lies so clever they sound like the truth. [15]Instead, we will speak the truth in love, growing in every way more and more like Christ, who is the head of his body, the church. NLT

Story: Safety in Boundaries

Kaboom!! The roll of thunder shook the ground violently as tens of thousands of Israelites fell on their faces to the ground. The small children held to their parents tightly. Crack, Boom! The mountain in front of them was a frightening display of dark rolling clouds, lightning, and deafening thunder. Just when the people of Israel were about to turn and run in fear someone spotted a figure descending from the mountain. It was Moses! Moses had been commanded by the Lord to mark off a boundary around the mountain that people or animals could not pass. The mountain was to be considered holy and must not be touched by the people until the appropriate time. If anyone or any animal passed the line before the appropriate time they would die.

If you were given the responsibility as Moses was given that day from the Lord what would you do? Do you know where the mountain begins? Does it begin at the valley floor or at a certain elevation? You better make sure that you are right because there are people that might die if you don't mark the boundary in the right place.

We are not given any information that Moses was told where God wanted the line to be drawn. Therefore, we might assume that wherever Moses saw fit to draw the line it would be honored by God and was ok with God. Men of God must still create boundaries and draw lines today. It is the work of God and the design of God that a leader makes decisions. Pastors must make decisions on a regular basis regarding worldly activities, entertainment, changes in technology, and secular ideas. His decision to make a boundary is not based upon his personal desires but it is based upon Godly principles and what is in the best interest of the people of God that they lead. It is also in the plan of God that people submit themselves to the decisions that men and women of God make in regards to where the boundaries are made.

Moses had a great responsibility that day he was told to draw a boundary. He had to ensure the safety of God's people while at the same time allowing them freedom to make personal choices. Your pastor has the same responsibility. Pray for them that God gives wisdom to draw lines and create boundaries where they need to be made for our safety and salvation.

 **Application**

Drawing a Line

1. Have a time of family prayer and devotion:
   - Start with praise and worship unto God.
   - Ask God to forgive you of any sin in your life.

2. Is there any area of your life where you are doing things that go against the teaching of God's Word or against the teachings of your Pastor?

3. Are there things you do that your Pastor has taught against or preached against that you do not agree with?
   - Why?
   - Do you understand the reason behind your Pastor teaching against such activities?

4. Pray God will help you live a life that is submitted to both God and the spiritual authority that God has placed in your life.

5. Pray for your pastor and his family that God would give them wisdom to lead the people of God.

6. Pray for any personal needs as a family together.

 **Family Activity**

Follow the Leader

Start with the oldest family member as the leader. Go all over the house and even outside if possible. Change leaders every few minutes until everyone has had a chance to be the leader.

Try to go places that are difficult for others to get through or over. Make sure that you help one another navigate the obstacles and difficult places.

Talk about how a Pastor's job is to help the people of God navigate through the difficult areas of life. His goal is not to leave people behind or put impossible obstacles in their way but to help as many people as possible make it to heaven.

Purity

 ## Scripture

Take turns reading the following scriptures out loud.

Psalm 86:11; Teach me your ways, O Lord, that I may live according to your truth! Grant me purity of heart, so that I may honor you. NLT

2 Corinthians 6:3-10; ³We live in such a way that no one will stumble because of us, and no one will find fault with our ministry. ⁴In everything we do, we show that we are true ministers of God. We patiently endure troubles and hardships and calamities of every kind. ⁵We have been beaten, been put in prison, faced angry mobs, worked to exhaustion, endured sleepless nights, and gone without food. ⁶We prove ourselves by our purity, our understanding, our patience, our kindness, by the Holy Spirit within us, and by our sincere love. ⁷We faithfully preach the truth. God's power is working in us. We use the weapons of righteousness in the right hand for attack and the left hand for defense. ⁸We serve God whether people honor us or despise us, whether they slander us or praise us. We are honest, but they call us impostors. ⁹We are ignored, even though we are well known. We live close to death, but we are still alive. We have been beaten, but we have not been killed. ¹⁰Our hearts ache, but we always have joy. We are poor, but we give spiritual riches to others. We own nothing, and yet we have everything. NLT

Story: 100% Pure

Purity: The condition or quality of being pure; freedom from anything that debases, contaminates, pollutes, etc. living according to the original design.

A farmer went each week to the Farmers' Market to sell the produce and goods that he made on his farm. Two of the items the farmer took with him were cottage cheese and apple butter. He carried these items in two large tubs. He used large ladles to scoop the two items from the big tub into smaller containers. One day he got to the market and realized that he had left one of the ladles at home. He felt he had no choice but to use the one he had for both the cottage cheese and the apple butter. With each dip of the ladle the farmer saw that the apple butter and the cottage cheese began to slowly mix. Before the farmers Market was over that night the farmer could no longer tell the two products apart. People would walk up to the farmer's booth and look into the tubs of cottage cheese and apple butter and say, "That doesn't look good! What is it?" The farmer realized that by allowing the contents of the two to mix he ruined them both.

That's the way it is when we try to live for God and still involve ourselves in the sinful activities of this world. When our righteousness is mixed with the filth and corruption of this world the result is, we are no longer pure as God desires us to be. When we entangle ourselves with the cares and desires of this world we become contaminated.

So how do we remain pure as God desires us to be? Paul says it best when he describes how the life of a Christian should behave when writing to the church in Corinth, "We prove ourselves by our purity, our understanding, our patience, our kindness, by the Holy Spirit within us, and by our sincere love. 7 We faithfully preach the truth. We use the weapons of righteousness in the right hand for attack and the left hand for defense. 8 We serve God whether people honor us or despise us, whether they slander us or praise us." Purity is living according to the original design. God designed us to serve and love Him, not to serve and love the things of this world. We do what is right regardless, because when we begin to allow wrong things into our lives we become just like the cottage cheese or the apple butter, so mixed up and contaminated that we are no longer any good.

 **Application**

Purity

1. Have a time of family prayer and devotion:
   - Start with praise and worship unto God.
2. Ask God to forgive you of any sin in your life and to purify your life back to the original design He created.
3. Ask God to renew a hunger for righteousness and holiness within you.
4. Pray for a spirit of purity to spread in your Sunday school, youth group, and church.
5. Pray for any personal needs as a family together.

 Family Activity

Biblical Hangman

- Start the game by having one person choose a word or phrase that the other player knows how to spell.
- Place one dash on the bottom of a piece of paper for each letter of the word or words chosen. Leave a space between words.
- Draw a "gallows" at the top of the paper - draw a horizontal line at the bottom, a vertical line coming up out of its center, and then a short line off to the right at the top (so that you now have an upside-down "L" on the horizontal line).
- Have the other player guess one letter at a time - he or she may use a turn to guess the entire word or words.
- Fill in the letter on the appropriate dash each time the person guesses correctly.
- Add one body part to the drawing each time the letter chosen is not in the word. Begin by drawing a head attached to the short vertical line. Add eyes, ears, nose, hair, body, legs, and arms.
- If the drawing of the person is completed before the word or words are guessed, the guessing player loses. If the player figures out the word or words first, he or she gets a point.

You can play as long as you want to!

Sacrifice

 ## Scripture

Take turns reading the following scriptures out loud.

Psalm 51:17; The sacrifice you desire is a broken spirit. You will not reject a broken and repentant heart, O God. NLT

Matthew 20:17-19; [17]As Jesus was going up to Jerusalem, he took the twelve disciples aside privately and told them what was going to happen to him. [18]"Listen," he said, "we're going up to Jerusalem, where the Son of Man will be betrayed to the leading priests and the teachers of religious law. They will sentence him to die. [19]Then they will hand him over to the Romans to be mocked, flogged with a whip, and crucified. But on the third day he will be raised from the dead." NLT

Story: The Old Rugged Cross

God robed himself in human flesh and blood to come to earth to pay a debt He didn't owe because we owed a debt we couldn't pay.

The sacrifice Jesus paid for our redemption is beautiful and powerful. What is troubling is how easy it is for us as His children to take what He did for granted. I'm not saying we don't appreciate what Jesus did for us, on the contrary, most of us are deeply moved by the beautiful act of love God did on our behalf. What I am saying is most of us take for granted the blood of the Lord Jesus. Taking something for granted = not fully appreciating and respecting something or someone because we have grown accustomed to it. God's blood is readily available for us each and every time we sin and fail God. What we don't realize is how precious that blood is and how painful the sacrifice was that He paid to ensure we could have forgiveness of sin.

Every year in Alaska a 1000-mile dogsled race is ran to commemorate a life and death race that was run by ordinary men who worked desperately to save the lives of their loved ones back in 1926. In January of 1926, six-year-old Richard Stanley showed symptoms of diphtheria, signaling the possibility of an outbreak in the small town of Nome. When the boy passed away a day later, Dr. Curtis Welch began immunizing children and adults with an experimental but effective anti-diphtheria serum. It wasn't long before Dr. Welch's supply ran out, and the nearest serum was in Nenana, Alaska--1000 miles of frozen wilderness away. Amazingly, a group of trappers and prospectors volunteered to cover the distance with their dog teams! Operating in relays from trading post to trapping station and beyond, one sled started out from Nome while another, carrying the serum, started from Nenana. Oblivious to frostbite, fatigue, and exhaustion, the teamsters mushed relentlessly until, after 144 hours in minus 50 degree winds, the serum was delivered to Nome. As a result, only one other life was lost to the potential epidemic. Their sacrifice gave an entire town the gift of life.

All of mankind was infected with a terrible disease of the soul. Without treatment it would be impossible for any of us to ever survive. There was a deep, dark, cavernous valley filled with all sorts of wicked and vile creatures at the bottom that separated humanity from the cure. God saw there was no man who would be able to cross the great divide, so He robed himself in flesh and blood and came and crossed the great uncross able wilderness. He made sure a bridge was built so a steady supply of this precious soul saving serum would always flow to those who need and want it. That bridge still stands to this day, and the cure continues to steadily pour from it to sinful humanity, providing an eternal cure. The cross stands as the symbol of that sacrifice to this very day.

If you were to look at Rembrandt's painting of The Three Crosses, your attention would be drawn first to the center cross on which Jesus died. Then as you look at the crowd gathered around the foot of that cross, you'd be impressed by the various facial expressions and actions of the people involved in the awful crime of crucifying the Son of God. Finally, your eyes would drift to the edge of the painting and catch sight of another figure, almost hidden in the shadows. Rembrandt recognized that it was for his sin that Jesus suffered and died on the old rugged cross, and he never wanted to take for granted the sacrifice that represents a love greater than anything we have ever experienced before.

Each one of us is in desperate need of that soul saving serum Christ gave to us over 2000 years ago. His blood shed upon the cross is what each and every one of us needs to save us from the sickness of sin. The precious blood is available to every man, woman, and child who asks God for His mercy and grace. What a wonderful sacrifice indeed!

 **Application**

Sacrifice

1. Have a time of family prayer and devotion:
   - Start with praise and worship unto God.
   - Ask God to forgive you of any sin in your life.

2. Pray God helps you to never take the sacrifice He paid on Calvary for granted.

3. Are there things or people in your life you take for granted?
   - If there are, you need to ask God to forgive you for not treating them with the respect and reverence you should have.

4. Pray for any personal needs as a family together.

 Family Activity

The Cross

- Purchase a box of Popsicle sticks from the craft store. (Get some glue too!)
- Build a cross using at least two Popsicle sticks, or more if you want to make it bigger.
- Write or paint the names of loved ones on the cross as a reminder that Jesus died for them.
- Take a few moments to pray for each name written upon the cross.
- Place the crosses somewhere they can be seen as a reminder to pray for the person whose name is written on the cross.

Safeguard Your Home

 **Scripture**
Take turns reading the following scriptures out loud.

Matthew 6:22-24; [22]Your eye is a lamp that provides light for your body. When your eye is good, your whole body is filled with light. [23]But when your eye is bad, your whole body is filled with darkness. And if the light you think you have is actually darkness, how deep that darkness is! [24]No one can serve two masters. For you will hate one and love the other; you will be devoted to one and despise the other. You cannot serve both God and money. NLT

Psalm 101:1-8; [1]I will sing of your love and justice, Lord. I will praise you with songs. [2]I will be careful to live a blameless life - when will you come to help me? I will lead a life of integrity in my own home. [3]I will refuse to look at anything vile and vulgar. I hate all who deal crookedly; I will have nothing to do with them. [4]I will reject perverse ideas and stay away from every evil. [5]I will not tolerate people who slander their neighbors. I will not endure conceit and pride. [6]I will search for faithful people to be my companions. Only those who are above reproach will be allowed to serve me. [7]I will not allow deceivers to serve in my house, and liars will not stay in my presence. [8]My daily task will be to ferret out the wicked and free the city of the Lord from their grip. NLT

Story: The Nature of Sin

The phone rings at the 911 call center in Florida. As the operator picks up the phone and answers, "911 how can we help you?", a frantic man screams out, "It's an emergency. I think the baby's dead."

Earlier that night when the 32 year-old father went to bed, he noticed his nine foot long Albino Burmese Python trying frantically to get out of its cage. The father had purchased the Python several years ago when it was a small, cute pet just a few feet long. As time went by and the man tended to feeding and caring for the snake, like all snakes, it grew in size and in danger. As the father went to bed that night, he tucked in his 2 year-old daughter, shut off the lights, and fell sleep.

When he awoke in the morning, he walked to the kitchen to grab his morning cup of coffee and noticed that the Python had managed to pry the top of the cage loose and escape. He frantically began to search the house for his pet snake. When he walked into his two year old daughter's room he gasped with horror. The 9-foot-long Python had made its way into the bed of the little girl and did what comes natural to all hungry Pythons; it wrapped itself around the 2 year old little girl as she lay in her bed and strangled her to death.

On the phone with the 911 operator, the father, barely able to communicate between sobs, told the operator that his Albino Burmese Python killed his baby girl. "Our pet snake got out in the middle of the night and strangled the baby!" he was heard crying. "Our snake strangled the baby!"

Isn't that what snakes do? The nature of a snake is to hunt and kill things that are vulnerable so it can eat and survive. You can tend to the needs of the creature by feeding and caring for it for years, but all your efforts will never change the true nature of the snake; it wants to strike and kill.

Too many people think they can control sin and evil, because after all, it does kind of look cute, and it is fun to have around to play with at times. They care for and feed sin and evil for years and take great efforts to keep it safe from others in the home, but eventually the nature of the beast will cause it to escape one day and do what it was created to do, kill. Sin and evil will always do what it has in its nature; steal, kill and destroy. Unfortunately the ones who get hurt the most are children who live in the home, not the parents who brought the creature home in the first place. Romans 6:23; For the wages of sin is death; but the gift of God is eternal life through Jesus Christ our Lord.

Safeguard Your Home

1. Have a time of family prayer and devotion:
   - Start with praise and worship unto God.
   - Ask God to forgive you of any sin in your life.

2. Is there anything in your home that may cause harm to someone else?
   - What steps should you take to make sure that no one gets hurt?
   - Should you get rid of that thing or things all together?

3. Is there anything we allow in our home because it is fun, but deep down inside we know within the nature of the beast is the desire to steal, kill and destroy our relationship with God?

4. Pray God will help you live a life of integrity in your own home, and that you will put nothing vile or vulgar in front of your eyes.

5. Pray for any personal needs as a family together.

 Family Activity

Monster Exterminator

- Choose one person to be the Exterminator.
- Everyone else in the family is a monster and must hide in various places throughout the house while the Monster Exterminator counts to 30.
- The Exterminator then must find each and every monster and touch them with his monster blaster (The Bible).
- The last monster to be found will be the Exterminator for the next game.

Scripture Memory

Scripture
Take turns reading the following scriptures out loud.

Deuteronomy 6:1-9; ¹These are the commands, decrees and laws the Lord your God directed me to teach you to observe in the land that you are crossing the Jordan to possess, ²so that you, your children and their children after them may fear the Lord your God as long as you live by keeping all his decrees and commands that I give you, and so that you may enjoy long life. ³Hear, O Israel, and be careful to obey so that it may go well with you and that you may increase greatly in a land flowing with milk and honey, just as the Lord, the God of your fathers, promised you. ⁴Hear, O Israel: The Lord our God, the Lord is one. ⁵Love the Lord your God with all your heart and with all your soul and with all your strength. ⁶These commandments that I give you today are to be upon your hearts. ⁷Impress them on your children. Talk about them when you sit at home and when you walk along the road, when you lie down and when you get up. ⁸Tie them as symbols on your hands and bind them on your foreheads. ⁹Write them on the doorframes of your houses and on your gates. KJV

Story: Thy Word Have I Hid in My Heart

In a small Russian village the local priest came up with a plan to increase attendance at Sunday school. The priest started handing out candy to the peasant children when they came to church and when they memorized the weekly scripture verse. One of the most faithful was a pug-nosed, aggressive lad who recited his scriptures with proper faithfulness, pocketed his reward, then fled into the fields to munch on it.

The priest took a liking to the boy, and persuaded him to attend church school. To the young man, this was a more preferable task than doing household chores from which his devout parents excused him. By offering weekly bribes, the priest managed to teach the boy the four Gospels. In fact, the boy eventually won a special prize for learning all four by heart and reciting them nonstop in church. Sixty years later, the boy still liked to recite scriptures, but in a context that would horrify the elderly priest who taught him. The prize pupil, who memorized so much of the Bible, was Nikita Khrushchev, the former Communist Czar. Nikita was directly responsible for many of the deaths in Russia during the Great Purge, a series of campaigns of political repression and murder in the Soviet Union orchestrated byJoseph Stalin from 1936 to 1939.

This story illustrates that the "why" behind scripture memorization is fully as important as the "what". Nikita Khrushchev who easily recited God's Word as a child, later declared God to be nonexistent. One of his reasons was that when Russian astronauts made it into space they were unable to see God. Khrushchev originally memorized the scriptures for the candy, the rewards, and bribes, rather than for the meaning it had for his life. The superficial motivation produced superficial results in Khrushchev, and it will have the same results in you if you don't fall in love with the one true living God!

In Deuteronomy 6, God commands Israel to commit themselves wholeheartedly to the commands He gave them. They were to continually repeat them to their children, talk about them whenever and wherever they had an opportunity and write the commands in places they would see every day. Why? God knew there would come a day when life would lead them away from Him. God tells Israel, "Be careful not to forget the Lord, who rescued you from slavery in the land of Egypt."

This command has not changed for you and I today. We have the responsibility to learn God's Word, and not just learn it but to love it! Learning the Word of God without loving the author of the Word will produce men and women with superficial relationships like Khrushchev. People like Khrushchev are only interested in knowing the Word of God so they can use it to get what they want. They never learn to let the Word mold and shape them into a vessel that brings honor and glory to God.

 ## Application

Scripture Memory

1. Have a time of family prayer and devotion
2. Read Psalm 106:1-5. Spend a few minutes thanking God for His blessings in your life.
3. Talk about a time or event in your life when you were especially thankful for God's Word.
4. Ask God to forgive you of any sin in your life.
5. Pray and ask God to put a love for Him and His Word in your life.
6. Pray for any personal needs as a family together.

 ## Family Activity

Bible Baseball

Set Up:
- You will need 4 bases - home plate, 1st base, 2nd base, and 3rd base. You will also need one card with the following titles - Home run, Single, Double, and Triple. Place the bases on the ground in baseball diamond fashion and place the cards in a bucket.

How to Play:
- Pick one person who will be the pitcher. The pitcher will think of and will ask the batter a Biblical question.
- If the batter gets it correct, they now get the chance to pick a card out of the bucket. If they pick the single card they move to first base, the double card moves them to second base, the triple card moves them to third base and the Home Run card gives them an automatic home run.
- Place the chosen card back into the bucket.
- Give everyone a chance to bat.
- See how many points you can score with everyone batting 2 or 3 times.

Start over again and see if you can beat your previous score.

Courage

Scripture

Take turns reading the following scriptures out loud.

Deuteronomy 31:6-8; [6]So be strong and courageous! Do not be afraid and do not panic before them. For the Lord your God will personally go ahead of you. He will neither fail you nor abandon you." [7]Then Moses called for Joshua, and as all Israel watched, he said to him, "Be strong and courageous! For you will lead these people into the land that the Lord swore to their ancestors he would give them. You are the one who will divide it among them as their grants of land. [8]Do not be afraid or discouraged, for the Lord will personally go ahead of you. He will be with you; he will neither fail you nor abandon you." NLT

Mark 6:47-51; [47]Late that night, the disciples were in their boat in the middle of the lake, and Jesus was alone on land. [48]He saw that they were in serious trouble, rowing hard and struggling against the wind and waves. About three o'clock in the morning Jesus came toward them, walking on the water. He intended to go past them, [49]but when they saw him walking on the water, they cried out in terror, thinking he was a ghost. [50]They were all terrified when they saw him. But Jesus spoke to them at once. "Don't be afraid," he said. "Take courage! I am here!" [51]Then he climbed into the boat, and the wind stopped. They were totally amazed. NLT

Story: Be Strong and Courageous

One morning as Ray Blankenship was preparing breakfast, he gazed out the window, and saw a small girl being swept along in the rain-flooded drainage ditch beside his Andover, Ohio, home. Ray knew that further downstream, the ditch disappeared with a roar underneath a road and then emptied into a series of large pipes that carried water underneath the city. Ray dashed out the door and raced along the ditch, trying to get ahead of the floundering child. Then he hurled himself into the deep, churning water. Blankenship surfaced and was able to grab the child's arm. They tumbled end over end. Within about three feet of the yawning culvert, Ray's free hand felt something, possibly a rock, protruding from one bank. He clung desperately, but the tremendous force of the water tried to tear him and the child away. "If I can just hang on until help comes," he thought. Ray did better than just hang on. By the time fire-department rescuers arrived, Ray had pulled the girl to safety. Both were treated for shock. On April 12, 1989, Ray Blankenship was awarded the Coast Guard's Silver Lifesaving Medal. The award is fitting, for this selfless courageous person was at even greater risk to himself than most people knew. Ray Blankenship does not know how to swim.

There are times in life when we will face challenges that require us to have and display courage. Sometimes the situation will come out of nowhere, like the story above, and we react with little thought. Other occasions present us with time to think about what action we will take. In those instances we must have courage to stand for what is right, regardless of the circumstance or the repercussions. We must always remember God is with us in any situation. As the disciples struggled in the little boat against the wind and waves, they were not afraid because they had been in similar circumstances. In fact, Jesus was going to walk right on by and continue to the other side until the disciples saw him and thought He was a ghost. Then they were terrified! Once Jesus realized they were afraid, He reassured them of His presence, "Don't be afraid. Take courage! I am here!" Then He came and got into the boat with them.

In our scripture, Joshua needed courage to face situations and trials in his life. Joshua had time to think about the problems he would face and he forced himself to be courageous in the face of difficult circumstances.

Whether the situation you face is an emergency or something in the future, remember God is with you and He is the source of your courage and strength!

 **Application**

Courage

1. Have a time of family prayer and devotion.
2. Spend time thanking God for His strength and power in your life that helps you be courageous.
3. Are there situations in your life right now you need courage in?
4. Pray God would help give you the courage you need to stand for what is right.
5. Pray for other people you know who need courage right now.

 **Family Activity**

Sharing Courage

Memorize: **Philippians 4:13;** I can do all things through Christ which strengtheneth me. KJV
Courage: the quality of mind or spirit that enables a person to face danger, fear, or difficulty.

- Share an experience in your life when you or someone you were with had to display courage.
- Ask the question: "Was the story that was shared an example of courage or foolishness? Courage and foolishness is not the same thing. Some people will do something foolish and say they just had the courage to do something that no one else would do.

Standing for Truth

 ## Scripture

Take turns reading the following scriptures out loud.

Proverbs 12:19-22; ¹⁹Truthful words stand the test of time, but lies are soon exposed. ²⁰Deceit fills hearts that are plotting evil; joy fills hearts that are planning peace! ²¹No harm comes to the godly, but the wicked have their fill of trouble. ²²The Lord detests lying lips, but he delights in those who tell the truth. NLT

1 John 3:18-22; ¹⁸Dear children, let's not merely say that we love each other; let us show the truth by our actions. ¹⁹Our actions will show that we belong to the truth, so we will be confident when we stand before God. ²⁰Even if we feel guilty, God is greater than our feelings, and he knows everything. ²¹Dear friends, if we don't feel guilty, we can come to God with bold confidence. ²²And we will receive from him whatever we ask because we obey him and do the things that please him. NLT

Story: Not Going To Bow

A few years ago a psychologist carried out an interesting experiment with teenagers designed to show how a person handles group pressure. The plan was simple. They brought groups of ten teenagers into a room for a test. Each group of ten was given instructions to raise their hands when the teacher pointed to the longest line on three separate charts. What one person in the group did not know was that nine of the others in the room had been instructed ahead of time to vote for the second-longest line. So regardless of the instructions they heard, once they were all together in the group, the nine were not to vote for the longest line, but rather vote for the next to the longest line. The experiment began with nine teen-agers voting for the wrong line. The one teen who didn't know what was going on would typically glance around, frown in confusion, and slip his hand up with the group. The instructions were repeated and the next card was raised. Time after time, the self-conscious teen would sit there saying a short line was longer than a long line, simply because they lacked courage to challenge the group. This remarkable conformity occurred in about 75% of the cases, and was true of small children and high-school students as well.

Conformity is defined as: doing and thinking as others, or behavior, or thought that is socially acceptable or expected. There is a deep desire within each one of us to belong or fit in with people or groups. No one likes to be the outcast or reject. We all want to fit in and just flow with what everyone else is doing around us. This is the pressure to conform. When no one notices us because we act or look just like everyone else around us, we have conformed to the expectations of society.

For Christians, there is a tremendous problem that arises when we fit in with everyone else. We are clearly commanded by Jesus to be the light to this world. Matthew 5:14; You are the light of the world—like a city on a hilltop that cannot be hidden. 15 No one lights a lamp and then puts it under a basket. Instead, a lamp is placed on a stand, where it gives light to everyone in the house. 16 In the same way, let your good deeds shine out for all to see, so that everyone will praise your heavenly Father. We have to stand out. We have to be different. How will anyone ever know we have what this lost and dying world is looking for if we look and act just like everyone else.

The Spirit of God gives us strength and power to stand for what is right even if we have to stand alone. The person in the research study who felt tremendous pressure to give the wrong answer, because everyone else was giving the wrong answer, is an example of the power of conformity. Conformity will cause you to believe what you know is a lie, and say that the lie is the truth, even if you know without a doubt it is wrong. You need to know right now that you never stand alone for any truth. When you are willing to speak the truth and stand for what is right, God always stands with you. When you conform to God's expectations you are always right. What God thinks always means more than what people think.

 <u>**Application**</u>

Standing for Truth

Have a time of family prayer and devotion:
1. Start by talking about the pressure to conform each family member deals with on a regular basis.
2. Do you have family members or close friends that make decisions or act only because they want to fit in with others?
3. Memorize 1 John 2:15-16; Love not the world, neither the things that are in the world. If any man love the world, the love of the Father is not in him. 16 For all that is in the world, the lust of the flesh, and the lust of the eyes, and the pride of life, is not of the Father, but is of the world.
4. Ask God to forgive you of sin in your life.
5. Pray God will help you stand for what is right, and not for what is popular.
6. Pray for personal needs as a family together.

 <u>**Family Activity**</u>

Penny Walk

Take a penny with you as you go for a walk around your neighborhood (actually any coin will do).

- When you come to a place where you have an option to go left or right flip the penny in the air and let it land: Heads = right turn, Tails = left turn.
- If you reach a place where you have to make a decision to either go back or keep going straight flip the penny: Heads = go straight, Tails = turn back. Let the Penny make the decisions for you as you take this walk.

Discuss how using a penny to choose your direction is like allowing the world to make decisions for you in life. Following the world does not usually make sense, and you don't always go in the direction you want or need to go. Most likely you will end up somewhere you really didn't want to be.

Thankfulness

 ## Scripture

Take turns reading the following scriptures out loud.

Colossians 3:16-17; [16]Let the message about Christ, in all its richness, fill your lives. Teach and counsel each other with all the wisdom he gives. Sing Psalm and hymns and spiritual songs to God with thankful hearts. [17]And whatever you do or say, do it as a representative of the Lord Jesus, giving thanks through him to God the Father. NLT

Story: Attitude of Gratitude

It is gratitude that prompted an elderly man to visit an old broken pier on the eastern seacoast of Florida. Every Friday night, until his death in 1973, he would return, walking slowly and slightly stooped with a large bucket of shrimp. The seagulls would flock to this old man, and he would feed them from his bucket. Many years before in October 1942, Captain Eddie Rickenbacker was on a mission in a B-17 to deliver an important message to General Douglas MacArthur in New Guinea, but there was an unexpected detour which would hurl Captain Eddie into the most harrowing adventure of his life.

Somewhere over the South Pacific the Flying Fortress became lost beyond the reach of radio. Fuel ran dangerously low, so the men ditched their plane in the ocean. For nearly a month Captain Eddie and his companions would fight the water, severe weather, and scorching sun. They spent many sleepless nights recoiling as giant sharks rammed their rafts. The largest raft was nine by five. The biggest shark . . . ten feet long.

Of all their enemies at sea, one proved most formidable; starvation. Eight days out, their rations were long gone or destroyed by salt water. It would take a miracle to sustain them. A miracle occurred. In Captain Eddie's own words, "Cherry," that was the B-17 pilot Captain William Cherry, "read the service that afternoon, and we finished with a prayer for deliverance and a hymn of praise. There was some talk, but it tapered off in the oppressive heat. With my hat pulled down over my eyes to keep out some of the glare, I dozed off."

"Something landed on my head. I knew it was a seagull. I don't know how I knew, I just knew. Everyone else knew too. No one said a word, but peering out from under my hat brim without moving my head, I could see the expression on their faces. They were staring at that gull. The gull meant food . . . if I could catch it."

Captain Eddie caught the seagull. Its flesh was eaten. Its intestines were used for bait to catch fish. The survivors were sustained and their hopes renewed because a lone seagull, uncharacteristically hundreds of miles from land, offered itself as a sacrifice.

This is why Captain Eddie never forgot about the seagulls, and every Friday evening, about sunset, on a lonely stretch along the eastern Florida seacoast you see an old man walking, white-haired, bushy-browed, and slightly bent. His bucket filled with shrimp was to feed gulls, to remember the one which on a day long past gave itself without a struggle, like manna in the wilderness.

A tremendous sacrifice was given for you approximately 2000 years ago when Jesus shed his blood on the cross to wash away sins of mankind. You can never repay Him for what He did for you, but you can start by being thankful. Do you ever stop and think what life would be like if our sin was not forgiven? How much guilt, condemnation, and pain would we have to carry with us each and every day because of our sinful actions? What would our life be like today if there was no hope of ever seeing God face to face in the heavenly realm? An old church song says it so clearly and precise:

Thank God for the blood,
Thank God for the blood,
Thank God for the blood,
That washes white as snow.

Ref.: Paul Aurandt, "*The Old Man and the Gulls*", Paul Harvey's *The Rest of the Story*, 1977.

Application

Thankfulness

1. Have a time of family prayer and devotion.
2. Start by talking about things you are thankful for. Direct your comments to people in your family
   - Example: "Mom, I'm thankful for the wonderful dinners you make."
3. Are there people in your life you take for granted? What value do these people add to your family?
4. Spend some time thanking God for all His blessings in your life. (family, friends, church, Word of God, Holy Spirit, etc.)
5. Ask God to forgive you of any sin in your life.
6. Pray God would bless those you are thankful for.
7. Pray God would help you be more thankful for everyday things and people in your life you may have a tendency to take for granted.
8. Pray for any personal needs as a family together.

Family Activity

What Am I Thankful For?

- One person starts by giving small clues about something or someone they are thankful for. Try not to give away to many descriptive clues that would easily give others the name of the item or identity of the person.
- The first person to either name the person or item the person is thankful for wins that round.
- The person who guesses correctly now gets to give clues for something or someone they are thankful for.
- Give each family member a chance to be the person who describes who or what they are thankful for.

The Power of The Blood

 ## Scripture

Take turns reading the following scriptures out loud.

Ephesians 1:3-10; [3]Praise be to the God and Father of our Lord Jesus Christ, who has blessed us in the heavenly realms with every spiritual blessing in Christ. [4]For he chose us in him before the creation of the world to be holy and blameless in his sight. In love [5]he predestined us to be adopted as his sons through Jesus Christ, in accordance with his pleasure and will [6]to the praise of his glorious grace, which he has freely given us in the One he loves. [7]In him we have redemption through his blood, the forgiveness of sins, in accordance with the riches of God's grace [8]that he lavished on us with all wisdom and understanding. [9]And he made known to us the mystery of his will according to his good pleasure, which he purposed in Christ, [10]to be put into effect when the times will have reached their fulfillment to bring all things in heaven and on earth together under one head, even Christ. NIV

Revelation 12:10-11; [10]And I heard a loud voice saying in heaven, Now is come salvation, and strength, and the kingdom of our God, and the power of his Christ: for the accuser of our brethren is cast down, which accused them before our God day and night. [11]And they overcame him by the blood of the Lamb, and by the word of their testimony; and they loved not their lives unto the death. KJV

Story: Thank God for The Blood

The last reference to the power of the blood of Jesus is found in Revelation 12:11; And they overcame Him by the blood of the Lamb, and by the word of their testimony; and they loved not their lives unto the death. The scripture reminds us His blood has the power to overcome all things, and enables those who have been washed in the blood of the Lamb to partake in that power. Baptism in the name of Jesus is the only thing that connects us to that precious, powerful, cleansing blood that was shed over 2000 years ago. There are at least 43 references to the blood of Christ in the New Testament, all of them testify to its great importance in the salvation and daily life of the born again believer. Judas, the disciple of the Lord who betrayed him with a kiss, spoke of it as "innocent blood" (Matthew 27:4). In 1 Peter 1:9; Peter called it "the precious blood of Christ, as of a Lamb without blemish and without spot." It is the cleansing blood in 1 John 1:7 and the washing blood in Revelation 1:5, emphasizing that it removes the guilt of our sins.

Numerous songs that are hallmarks of the early Christian movement made reference to the blood of Jesus. In fact, there are many songs that reference only the precious blood of the Lamb, Jesus Christ. The following song is a classic that has been sung in church services for decades:

The blood that Jesus shed for me,
Way back on Calvary;
The blood that gives me strength
From day to day,
It will never lose its power.
It reaches to the highest mountain,
It flows to the lowest valley;
The blood that gives me strength
From day to day,
It will never, never lose its power.

When was the last time you sang a song that mentioned the blood of Jesus? Some people say that songs that reference the blood are offensive, crude, and should not be sung in our church services anymore. Others will say that references to the blood of Jesus might cause fear in children. What is scary is people who live life without the power of the blood of Jesus; that's what children and people should be afraid of. It's the blood that gives us power to overcome; power to rise above darkness of this world, desires of this flesh, and become what God desires us to be. Thank God for the Blood!

Application

The Power of The Blood

1. Have a time of family prayer and devotion.
2. Everyone thank God for His precious blood He shed back on Calvary for you.
3. Talk about a time or event in your life when you were especially thankful for God's blood.
4. Ask God to forgive you of any sin in your life.
5. Pray for people in your life that need the blood of Jesus to wash their sins away in baptism.
6. Pray for any personal needs as a family together.

Family Activity

Song Night

- With everyone sitting in the same room take turns singing church songs that have the word 'Blood" in it.
- Sing only a few lines and then let the person to your right go next. If the person is unable to sing a song with the word blood in it they are out. The last person remaining is the winner.
- The winner will then teach one or two songs that reference the Blood of Jesus to the entire family.
- Take the time to teach these wonderful songs to your family. There will come a day when you are thankful that your children understand the blessing of being washed in the blood and are thankful for that precious, soul saving, overcoming blood.

A Spirit of Giving

 ## Scripture

Take turns reading the following scriptures out loud.

Proverbs 11:25; A generous person will prosper; whoever refreshes others will be refreshed. NIV

2 Corinthians 9:6-11; [6]Remember this: Whoever sows sparingly will also reap sparingly, and whoever sows generously will also reap generously. [7]Each of you should give what you have decided in your heart to give, not reluctantly or under compulsion, for God loves a cheerful giver. [8]And God is able to bless you abundantly, so that in all things at all times, having all that you need, you will abound in every good work. [9]As it is written: "They have freely scattered their gifts to the poor; their righteousness endures forever." [10]Now he who supplies seed to the sower and bread for food will also supply and increase your store of seed and will enlarge the harvest of your righteousness. [11]You will be enriched in every way so that you can be generous on every occasion, and through us your generosity will result in thanksgiving to God. NIV

Story: Generous Heart

I am sure you have heard it said, "It is better to give than to receive." Many people automatically assume when someone uses the word "giving" the person is talking about money. However, there are many other ways someone can give besides just giving money. You can give of your time, skills, energy, possessions, and experience. People who give of themselves to serve others usually have a generous heart. Meaning, they enjoy helping other people just for the pure joy of seeing someone else happy. Individuals who "volunteer" their time to minister at the church because they want to serve God and be a blessing to others is an example of someone with a giving spirit. What a wonderful and generous thing to do with your time and ability; especially when you give and expect nothing in return! You see, giving with the expectation of getting something in return is not truly giving with a generous heart. Giving what is left over at the end of the day is not giving your best. The following poem describes this type of giving:

Leftovers are such humble things,
We would not serve to a guest,
And yet we serve them to our Lord
Who deserve the very best.
We give to Him leftover time,
Stray minutes here and there.
Leftover cash we give to Him,

Such few coins as we can spare.
We give our youth unto the world,
To hatred, lust and strife;
Then in declining years we give
To him the remnant of our life.

A person with a generous heart enjoys giving in all areas, but not everyone has a generous heart. Some people really struggle when it comes to giving. They understand the concept of giving but have a hard time being a joyful giver. One Sunday a mother wanted to teach her daughter a lesson about being generous. She gave the little girl a quarter and a dollar for church. "Put whichever one you want in the collection plate and keep the other for yourself," she told the girl. When they were coming out of church, the mother asked her daughter which amount she had given. "Well," said the little girl, "I was going to give the dollar, but just before the collection the man in the pulpit said we should all be cheerful givers. I knew I'd be a lot more cheerful if I gave the quarter, so I did." When it comes to being generous, God wants us to give because we trust Him, love Him, are obedient to Him, and because we want to be a blessing to others. Remember, no matter how much you give, you can never out give God.

Ref.: *Bits & Pieces*, February 4, 1993

 **<u>Application</u>**

A Spirit of Giving

1. Talk about the ways each family member or the family as a whole can be generous with their time, talents, and possessions to others.
2. Have a time of family prayer and devotion:
   - Start with thanksgiving and praise unto God.
   - Ask God to forgive you of any sin in your life.
3. If you struggle with having a generous attitude pray that God would help you learn through the process of obedience to have a generous heart.
   - The Bible states that obedience is better than sacrifice, and for those who struggle with generosity, often times obedience to God and His Word is the first step in having a generous heart.
4. Pray God would direct you to someone in need that you can bless.
5. Pray for any personal needs as a family together.

 **<u>Family Activity</u>**

A Blessing to Others

Choose one of the following items below and bless someone else:

- Everyone join in and make a dozen or more cookies or brownies. Place them on a pretty plate and take them to your neighbor(s). Your neighbor can be anyone who lives next to you or someone in your church that you want to be a blessing to.
- Go through a local drive-through and pay for the person behind you. Hand the person at the window a church invitation card to give to the person whose food you paid for. Pull forward just enough to see the look on their face when they realize you paid for their order. Drive off knowing you were a blessing to someone else.
- Wash the car of a neighbor, church member, grandparent etc.

Warfare Prayer

 ## Scripture

Take turns reading the following scriptures out loud.

James 5:16; Confess your faults one to another, and pray one for another, that ye may be healed. The effectual fervent prayer of a righteous man availeth much. KJV

1 Corinthians 10:4; For the weapons of our warfare are not carnal, but mighty through God to the pulling down of strong holds; KJV

John 10:10; The thief does not come except to steal, and to kill, and to destroy. I have come that they may have life, and that they may have it more abundantly. NKJV

Story: Devil Get Out of Here

Some people don't like to talk very much about spiritual warfare, because sometimes it can be kind of scary. Other times people like to blame the devil and spiritual warfare for everything bad that happens to them. At times we may be experiencing what "feels" like spiritual warfare and it is really God trying to get our attention and divert us back to the path of the straight and narrow. A wise pastor once said, "If you are doing everything that you know is right and bad things keep happening, then maybe you are dealing with spiritual warfare. However, if you are NOT doing everything that you know is right, then it is probably God trying to get your attention to get you back on track! This is a great tool to help discern warfare!

Sometimes as children of God we can be targeted by the devil because he wants to stop us from advancing and working for God. Several months ago there was a time of intense frustration in our home. It seemed as if no one even liked each other or could even get along. Tempers were raging, patience was thin, and for the most part no one in the family could even identify what was really wrong. That night I went to bed and the Lord allowed me to see spiritually what was taking place in our home. As I was sleeping I dreamt that a HUGE snake was in my bed lying directly between my husband and myself. When I woke up, I shared the dream with my husband and we realized that all the unusual intense frustration in our home was nothing more than spiritual warfare. The enemy had launched an attack against our home. That night we had our Monday night Family Devotion and my husband shared with our children that the frustration we were experiencing in our home was nothing more than an attack from Satan. He continued, "That the reason Satan is trying to wreak havoc in our home is because your Daddy is a man of God and Mommy is a women of God and the enemy's goal is to steal, kill and destroy." Well that night we prayed and sent the devil on the run! We took spiritual authority through tongue talking warfare prayer! As my husband laid across the floor praying, each child came and laid across his back and prayed in tongues as if to say NO WAY DEVIL - NOT MY HOME- NOT MY FAMILY! DEVIL GET AWAY FROM OUR HOME.

When the devil comes knocking at the door of your home, just remember the devil is not God's opposite he is much lower. He was kicked out of heaven along time ago and was already defeated at Calvary. We have the authority and power in the Name of Jesus to pray him away from our home!

 ## Application

Warfare Prayer

1. Talk about times where each family member has experienced warfare.
2. Do you feel like you could be experiencing warfare right now? Or is God trying to get your attention to get you back on track?
3. Have a time of family prayer:
   - Begin by praising God that He has given us all the power through the Name of Jesus to defeat the devil.
4. Ask God to forgive you of any sin in your life.
5. With fervency of prayer rebuke the attacks of Satan against your home and against your loved ones.
6. Pray that God would cover your home and family in the blood of Jesus.
7. End with thanking God for giving you and your family victory through the power of His blood.

 ## Family Activity

Devil Bashing Testimony Time

Revelation 12:11; And they overcame him by the blood of the Lamb, and by the word of their testimony… KJV

There is POWER in our testimony!

Have each family member get a testimony ready! Think of a time that God helped you through a particular situation or helped you resist temptation. Every time you give glory to Jesus through your testimony it's like you socked the devil right in the face! Go for it, I dare you to beat the Devil up real good!!

Important Decisions

Scripture

Take turns reading the following scriptures out loud.

Joshua 24:14-15; ¹⁴Now fear the Lord and serve him with all faithfulness. Throw away the gods your forefathers worshiped beyond the river and in Egypt, and serve the Lord. ¹⁵But if serving the Lord seems undesirable to you, then choose for yourselves this day whom you will serve, whether the gods your forefathers served beyond the river, or the gods of the Amorites, in whose land you are living. But as for me and my household, we will serve the Lord. NIV

2 Corinthians 6:14-16; ¹⁴Do not be yoked together with unbelievers. For what do righteousness and wickedness have in common? Or what fellowship can light have with darkness? ¹⁵What harmony is there between Christ and Belial? Or what does a believer have in common with an unbeliever? ¹⁶What agreement is there between the temple of God and idols? For we are the temple of the living God. As God has said: "I will live with them and walk among them, and I will be their God, and they will be my people." NIV

Colossians 3:17; And whatever you do, whether in word or deed, do it all in the name of the Lord Jesus, giving thanks to God the Father through him. NIV

Story: Decisions, Decisions, Decisions

As we begin to talk about decision making we must always remember to make decisions based upon what the Word of God says is right. We cannot go off of feelings but rather what is right. Wise decisions will always be accompanied with honesty, integrity, character, work ethic, and authority.

We are going to talk about 3 of the greatest decisions you will ever make in your life. It's important to get these three right because your quality of life will greatly depend on what choices you make. Yes, there are many more important decisions along the way, but these three are ones that provide the foundation, and key direction in one's life.

The first decision is choosing salvation. Making Jesus your number one priority in life. This means being baptized in the precious name of Jesus and receiving the gift of the Holy Ghost. Salvation is the most important decision in ones life, it will greatly affect your quality of life, presently, and in the life hereafter.

The second important decision in life is who you will marry. Lives are destroyed through marital strife and divorces. Many people have unfortunately seen first hand the heartache involved when two people are unequally yoked together in marriage. For a Christian, it is so important and biblical not to become married to an unbeliever. Having the same goals, objectives and values in life is a necessary part of marital success. It is better to remain unmarried than be married to the wrong person. Learn at an early age to listen to those in authority over your life, your pastor, your parents, and those that have your best interest at heart.

The third important decision is what one does for a vocation, i.e., what you do to earn a living. The wise old saying is, "If you do what you love, you will never have to work a day in your life" because you enjoy what you do. Young people should consider what they really are interested in doing. Once you figure out what career you are interested in, try to find an opportunity to actually do some type of work in that field. You will probably have to volunteer your time, but what better way to determine if you really like that type of work enough to spend the rest of your working years doing that job. One who really enjoys working on cars may be called to be a mechanic. One who really enjoys working with children may be called to be a teacher. Check the desire, pray, and pursue. Remember we can plan our steps but God will order them! If we do our part God will do His.

 **Application**

Important Decisions

A very popular business author once said, "A failure to plan, is a plan to fail." For some of you this topic may seem a bit premature but it is never too soon to start planting seeds into our children. If they grow up knowing what the expectations are for them they are more likely to follow through with these expectations. Thus, the seed planted early is more likely to grow deep roots and produce a bountiful harvest of blessings.

1. Have a time of family prayer and devotion:
   - Start with praise and worship to God.
   - Everyone at the same time repent of any sin in your life, wrong thoughts, bad attitudes, wrong words, etc.

2. Ask God to plant seeds of righteousness into your children's spirit that will help them make right decisions as they get older.

3. Parents pray that God would help you be an example of a good parent/spouse. Your children will look for someone like you when they get older.

4. Ask God to give you wisdom. James 1:5; If any of you lacks wisdom, you should ask God, who gives generously to all without finding fault, and it will be given to you.

5. Praise God for hearing your prayers. Thank Him in advance that He is helping your children make wise decisions.

 **Family Activity**

Mad, Sad and Glad

Get some of your favorite cookies ready, (baked or store bought) pour some milk, and everyone sit down at the table together. As you munch on your tasty treat, have a round table discussion.

- Go around the table and have each person share something from their day or week that made them mad.
- Go around the table again and have each person share something from their day or week that made them sad.
- Have each person share something from their day or week that made them glad!
- Ask the question; was it the decisions of another person that affected your mood?

Remember we are all affected not only by our own decisions, but also by the decisions of others. Make wise choices – Your affecting someone!

Fear Not

Scripture

Take turns reading the following scriptures out loud.

The "Fear Not" of Immediate Obedience: **Matthew 1:18-21;** [18]Now the birth of Jesus Christ was on this wise: When as his mother Mary was espoused to Joseph, before they came together, she was found with child of the Holy Ghost. [19]Then Joseph her husband, being a just man, and not willing to make her a public example, was minded to put her away privily. [20]But while he thought on these things, behold, the angel of the Lord appeared unto him in a dream, saying, Joseph, thou son of David, fear not to take unto thee Mary thy wife: for that which is conceived in her is of the Holy Ghost. [21]And she shall bring forth a son, and thou shalt call his name JESUS: for he shall save his people from their sins.

Story: God Is in Control

Would Joseph be criticized for his decision? Yes.

Would Joseph face ridicule and possibly rejection? Yes.

We never hear much about Joseph, but we do know he was a good man willing to follow the Word and direction of God regardless of the consequences. His faith and trust in God allowed him to see past difficulties of fleshly and worldly consequences and respond out of obedience.

The "Fear Not" of Salvation: Luke 2:10,11; "And the angel said unto them, Fear not: for, behold, I bring you good tidings...which shall be to all people. For unto you is born this day in the city of David a Savior, which is Christ the Lord."

If our greatest need had been information, God would have sent us an educator; If our greatest need had been technology, God would have sent us a scientist; If our greatest need had been money, God would have sent us an economist; If our greatest need had been pleasure, God would have sent us an entertainer; But our greatest need was forgiveness, so God sent us a Savior.

God is still in the soul saving business. The reason for His coming over 2000 years ago is still the reason for His moving today. It is not His desire that any should perish, but that all would come to repentance.

The "Fear Not" of the Humanly Impossible: Luke 1:26-35; God sent the angel Gabriel to Nazareth, a village in Galilee, [27]to a virgin named Mary. She was engaged to be married to a man named Joseph, a descendant of King David. [28]Gabriel appeared to her and said, "Greetings, favored woman! The Lord is with you!" [29]Confused and disturbed, Mary tried to think what the angel could mean. [30]"Don't be afraid, Mary," the angel told her, "for you have found favor with God! [31]You will conceive and give birth to a son, and you will name him Jesus. [32]He will be very great and will be called the Son of the Most High. The Lord God will give him the throne of his ancestor David. [33]And he will reign over Israel forever; his Kingdom will never end!" [34]Mary asked the angel, "But how can this happen? I am a virgin." [35]The angel replied, "The Holy Spirit will come upon you, and the power of the Most High will overshadow you. So the baby to be born will be holy, and he will be called the Son of God.

God still specializes in the impossible. You may be facing situations today that appear impossible. Have faith in God to be the one who makes a way when it seems like there is no way.

The "Fear Not" of Unanswered Prayer: Luke 1:13; "Fear not, Zacharias: for thy prayer is heard; and thy wife Elizabeth shall bear thee a son, and thou shalt call his name John"

Zacharias and Elizabeth were past their prime and had been praying for years for a child. In fact, when the answer came to Zacharias, he could not believe it and therefore the angel of the Lord made him mute until the day the child was to be named.

Fear not for God has heard your prayer: He is not deaf or hard of hearing, His arm is not short and his promise not slack that He cannot move on your behalf. He is a prayer answering God. Try Him and see that He is faithful and true. Fear Not: Be persistent in your prayers, God is still: A deliverer of the lost, a friend that sticks closer than a brother, a provider to His children, and an ever present help in time of need.

When Jesus was born on this earth, He came to remove fear from the heart of His people and replace it with Hope.

 **Application**

Fear Not

1. Have a time of family prayer and devotion.
2. Begin by thanking God for the Hope He brought to our lives by coming to this earth.
3. Pray His Spirit would help us have faith and not be afraid in the following areas:
   - Obedience to His Word.
   - Salvation
   - His ability to open doors that appear to be humanly impossible.
   - His ability to answer prayer.
4. Pray for each other one at a time:
   - Each family member share one personal prayer request, and one prayer request for someone else who is not in your family devotion.
5. End with praising and thanking God for bringing us Hope.

 Family Activity

Whistle Karaoke

- Divide the family into two teams. The goal of the game is to be the first team to successfully guess 5 Christmas Carols correctly.
- Flip a coin to see which team goes first. The winning team will choose one team member to whistle a Christmas Carol. The person who is chosen can't let anyone else know what song they have chosen.
- Both teams are free to shout out the name of the song once the whistling has begun.
- The team who correctly guesses the song gets one point and a member of their team will be the next person to whistle another Christmas Carol.
- The game continues until one team has 5 points.

  Mix up the teams for different results. If someone can't whistle let them hum.

Traditions

Scripture

Take turns reading the following scriptures out loud.

Mark 7: 5-13; [5]"So the Pharisees and teachers of religious law asked him, "Why don't your disciples follow our age-old tradition? They eat without first performing the hand-washing ceremony." [6]Jesus replied, "You hypocrites! Isaiah was right when he prophesied about you, for he wrote, 'These people honor me with their lips, but their hearts are far from me. [7]Their worship is a farce, for they teach man-made ideas as commands from God.' [8]For you ignore God's law and substitute your own tradition."

[9]Then he said, "You skillfully sidestep God's law in order to hold on to your own tradition. [10]For instance, Moses gave you this law from God: 'Honor your father and mother,' and 'Anyone who speaks disrespectfully of father or mother must be put to death.' [11]But you say it is all right for people to say to their parents, 'Sorry, I can't help you. For I have vowed to give to God what I would have given to you.' [12]In this way, you let them disregard their needy parents. [13]And so you cancel the word of God in order to hand down your own tradition. And this is only one example among many others." NLT

Story: Family Traditions

In 1903 the Russian Czar noticed a soldier posted for no apparent reason on Kremlin grounds. Every day, from sun up until sun down, the sentry stood in one specific spot. He inquired of the military commanders the purpose of the sentry. They discovered that in 1776 Catherine the Great found on that spot the first flower of spring. "Post a sentry here," she commanded, "so that no one tramples that flower under foot!" 127 years later, the sentry was still posted in the exact spot for reasons unknown to most. Some traditions are created by people blindly following what others required or did before them. It may not make sense, but because someone important established it, people assume it must be the right thing to do.

A very poor holy man lived in a remote part of China. Every day before meditation and prayer, in order to show his devotion, he put a dish of butter on the windowsill; an offering to his God. This was a meaningful symbol in that time since food was scarce. One day during his prayer time, his cat came in and ate the butter. To stop the cat from eating the butter, he began to tie the cat to the bedpost each day before his quiet time. The man was so respected for his faithfulness that others joined him as disciples to worship as he did. Generations later, long after the holy man had passed, his followers continued to place an offering of butter on the windowsill during prayer and meditation. Furthermore, each one bought a cat and tied it to a bedpost.

Do you and your family have traditions? Do you know who started the family tradition? Sometimes it's good to ask a few questions about old traditions: Why do we do this? Who started it? What is the purpose? Some traditions are valuable and well worth keeping. Other traditions may need to be updated to maintain their effectiveness in passing on family or Biblical values. It is very important we never place traditions above the Word of God. Jesus himself became upset when people did this, He said in Mark 7; "These people honor me with their lips, but their hearts are far from me, Their worship is a farce, for they teach man-made ideas as commands from God. 8 For you ignore God's law and substitute your own tradition." 9 Then he said, "You skillfully sidestep God's law in order to hold on to your own tradition." Make sure God's Word is the foundation of your family tradition.

Application

Traditions

1. Talk about family traditions you have in your home.

2. Are there traditions that don't make sense or no longer have relevance?

3. Have a time of family prayer:
   - Begin with thanksgiving and praise.
   - Ask God to forgive you of sin.
   - Ask God to reveal to you traditions that may have taken the place of what His Word says.

4. Ask God to help you live life according to His Word and not by man made traditions.

5. Pray and ask God to direct you to start a family tradition that honors both His Word and strengthens family values.

6. Take time and pray for the needs of each family member.

Family Activity

Create Your Own Family Tradition

Create a new family tradition you can implement this next holiday.
Examples:
- At Christmas when you give someone a gift, tell them why they are special to you and why you want to be a blessing to them at Christmas by giving them a gift. The words spoken have the possibility of meaning so much more than the actual gift.
- At Thanksgiving as everyone gathers around the table for the Thanksgiving meal, have everyone express what they are thankful for this past year.

The sky is the limit with traditions. Create a new tradition that can be passed on from generation to generation.

Precious Time

Scripture

Take turns reading the following scriptures out loud.

Psalm 90:12; Teach us to realize the brevity of life, so that we may grow in wisdom. NLT

Psalm 39: 4-7; [4]"Lord, remind me how brief my time on earth will be. Remind me that my days are numbered—how fleeting my life is. [5] You have made my life no longer than the width of my hand. My entire lifetime is just a moment to you; at best, each of us is but a breath." [6] We are merely moving shadows, and all our busy rushing ends in nothing. We heap up wealth, not knowing who will spend it. [7] And so, Lord, where do I put my hope? My only hope is in you. NLT

Story: How Are You Spending Your Time?

How would you like to spend two years making phone calls to people who are not home? Sound absurd? According to a time management study, that's how much time the average person spends trying to return calls to people who never seem to be home or who don't answer our call. The same research shows that we will spend six months waiting for traffic lights to turn green, another eight months reading junk mail, one year looking for misplaced objects, four years doing housework, five years waiting in line, and six years eating. These statistics should cause us to take a serious look at how we spend our time.

Imagine if you had a bank that credited your account each morning with $86,000 that carried over no balance from day to day, allowed you to keep no cash in your account, and every evening canceled whatever part of the amount you failed to use during the day. What would you do? You would use every dollar each and every day and use it to your advantage! Well you do have such a bank, and its name is TIME! Every morning it credits you with 86,400 seconds. Every night it rules off as lost whatever amount of time you failed to invest wisely. It carries over no balances, it allows no overdrafts. Each day it opens a new account with you. If you fail to use the days deposits, the loss is yours. There is no going back, and there is no borrowing from tomorrows balance.

Psalm 39 gives us a perspective on time. In David's complaint to God, he said, "You have made my life no longer than the width of my hand. My entire lifetime is just a moment to you; at best, each of us is but a breath." (v. 5). David is saying that in comparison to eternity our time on earth is really short. God does not want us to waste this valuable time that He has given to us. When we do waste the time God has given to us we throw away one of the most precious commodities we have. Each minute is a gift, a small piece of eternity. Sure, we have to make phone calls, wait at traffic lights, stand in line, and take the time to eat, but what about the rest of our time? Are we using it wisely or are we wasting it away doing things that will never make a difference in eternity.

"Time is the coin of your life. It is the only coin you have, and only you can determine how it will be spent. Be careful lest you let other people spend it for you." –Carl Sandburg.

Ref.: Survey of 6000 people polled in 1988, *U.S. News and World Report*, Jan 30, 1989, p. 81.

Application

Precious Time

1. Talk about the things you do as individuals that might be considered a waste of time.
2. Discuss how you can take a portion of each day and dedicate it to the Lord.
3. Have a time of family prayer and devotion:
    - Start with thanksgiving and praise unto God.
    - Ask God to forgive you of any sin in your life.
4. If you struggle with wasting time doing things that have no long term value in life pray that God would help you learn how to be a wise manager of the time He has given you.
5. Pray God would help you to have a right attitude when it comes to spending the precious coin called time.
6. Pray for any personal needs you may have one family member at a time.

Family Activity

Time Challenges

Complete the following three time challenges. The person with the overall fastest combined time is the winner.

You will need a piece of paper and a timer. Write down the times for each event and total them at the conclusion.

- Run around the outside of the house.
- Clean up their bedroom (All clothes and toys picked up off the floor and put away, bed made correctly).
- Starting with a closed Bible, find and read the following scriptures:
    - Psalm 90:12
    - Luke 12:37
    - Revelation 3:11-12
- Everyone over 12 years must find all three; those between 7-12 years must find two; those 6 years and younger need to find one.

The winner of the time challenge gets to pick dessert!